EFFECTIVE COMMUNICATION IN BUSINESS

Listening and Speaking Strategies, Dialog

Skills to Have Success in Your Business

George Ratson

Respective authors own all copyrights not held by the publisher.

The information herein is offered for informational purposes solely and is universal as so. The presentation of the information is without contract or any type of guarantee assurance.

The trademarks that are used are without any consent, and the publication of the trademark is without permission or backing by the trademark owner. All trademarks and brands within this book are for clarifying purposes only and are owned by the owners themselves, not affiliated with this document.

The trademarks that are utilized are with no assent, and the publication of the trademark is without consent or sponsorship by the

CONTENTS

Introduction 1

C's Of Effective Business Communication 5

Tips For Improving Your Business Communication
Skills 12

Why Better Communication Skills Lead To More
Sales Success 18

Great Communication Is Significant To Deals
Success. 23

Approaches To Build Consumer Trust Naturally 38

Communication Tips That Will Boost Customer
Trust 53

Powerful Business Communication Techniques 60

Successful Business Communication: 61

A Brief Overview Of The Different Types Of
Communication 81

What Is Effective Business Communication And
Why Is It Important? 85

Step By Step Instructions To Develop Effective Business Communication Skills................92

Key Standards Of Business Communication..........100

Comprehend Your Group Of Spectators 102

Make Progress Toward Clearness 103

Comprehend The Setting Of Your Communication103

Have An Unmistakable Reason As A Top Priority104

Select The Most Proper Medium..........................105

Salesforce Essentials, The New Way To Private Company Growth. 106

Communication Isolates A Decent Business From An Extraordinary One..119

Make Progress Through Effective Business Communication..121

Powerful Communication Means Business Success 125

The Requirement For Communication Aptitudes126

Communication Capacity Can Bring About Better Possibility Of Advancement 127

Preparing Workers In Communication For Improved Profitability..................................129

Brilliant Tips To Improve Communication In The Workplace...131

Characteristics Of Effective Business Communication...160

The Effects Of Poor Communication In Business 170

Representative Engagement Begins With Communications..195

Job Of Internal Communications In Business Strategy..208

The Business Strategy In Real Life.....................210

The Hazards Of Poor Communication................212

The Importance Of Communicating Business Strategy Effectively...213

Accomplishing Strategic Alignment....................215

Sharpening Communications Strategy 218

Myths About Effective Business Communication.220

The Challenges Of Business Communication........237

Conclusion 247

INTRODUCTION

It's about reality.

Have you, at any point, heard that articulation?

It's at the core of each business. The "main concern" is an organization's net gain after the sum total of what costs have been paid out of its profit. This primary concern decides if you remain in business. Also, without successful communication, you won't. Regardless of whether you're maintaining your very own business or simply beginning on your business vocation, you have to be an incredible communicator!

As indicated by an ongoing report, organizations with great communication practices are three and a half times bound to outflank their competitors. A business' capacity to contend might be the main motivation to advance successful communication, yet it's not alone.

Great communication manufactures great groups. When group pioneers are powerful communicators, they motivate laborers to go after a shared objective. They ensure everybody realizes their duties and how to perform them. With an open discourse, representatives contribute when others in the association need their assistance, and realize when to request help, consequently.

You can avert misconceptions with great communication. Bits of gossip and awful will can crash an association. Somebody says something, and another person disapproves. In any case, when there's transparent communication, everybody's in agreement. Certainly, there might be contradictions, yet they're more averse to transform into issues when differences of feeling are given the outlet and regard they merit.

Client assistance depends on great communication. If you don't have the foggiest idea what your clients need, how might you offer it to them? Regardless of whether you sell items or administrations, you have to tune in to the requirements of your clients, answer their inquiries, and give answers that sound good to them. What's more, when clients go to web-based life to convey, you should be brisk, mindful, and neighborly.

Great communication abilities will enable you to accomplish. Become a successful communicator and you'll not just support your organization; you'll help yourself. Having the option to convey well—recorded as a hard copy and in discourse— will separate you from your companions. It will enable you to exceed expectations at work and be perceived for your achievements and give you a focused edge in the activity showcase.

C'S OF EFFECTIVE BUSINESS COMMUNICATION

Cerebrum spasms can sneak up on anybody toward the finish of a difficult day of consistent communication. As the annoying cousin of a mental obstacle, which incidentally denies somebody of the capacity to make sense of what to state, mind issues stifle somebody's capacity to choose how to state it. When you're an entrepreneur whose occupation relies upon compelling business communication, this is one issue you have to cleanse in a rush. Alluding to the seven C's of business communication can help - particularly if you pair them with an apt update about why they matter.

1. Powerful Business Communication Is Clear

Anybody can turn into an accidental associate from a cerebrum spasm if that individual attempts to "sloppy up" a message with pointless convention and a couple of supposed twenty-dollar words. As much as you may wish to dazzle, recollect that the abrogating objective of communication is to ensure that you are comprehended. Clearness is recognized by unequivocal short sentences and solid words– of the five-dollar assortment. They're as yet extremely valuable

2. Compelling Business Communication Is Complete

No entrepreneur needs to be misjudged or told that he "overlooked" to add something to a report. It requires retreating, which can be a titanic time-squanderer. Generally, fragmented communication isn't the consequence of somebody not knowing or not having data, however, is normally the aftereffect of choosing that something wasn't important to incorporate. You can maintain a strategic distance from this entanglement by keeping your crowd top-of-mind. If you can't picture their needs and needs, decide in favor of including more data - as opposed to less.

3. Compelling Business Communication Is Concise

Of all your business communication systems, it presumably encourages most to put yourself in the job of the recipient. Indeed: When you open an email, content or letter, or you hear that somebody needs to talk with you, you likely need to know: "What do you need from me?" Being compact necessitates that you to arrive at the point rapidly while maintaining a strategic distance from superfluous tedium, "over-talking" and redundancy. Succinct messages are not just additionally engaging - they're likewise progressively critical.

4. Compelling Business Communication Is Concrete

Consider solid communication as the cousin of lucidity and concision. Often, solid communication is fortified by certainties, figures, delineations and models — anything that can help clarify a message with the goal that it isn't misconstrued. It leaves nothing to possibility and less to the creative mind. Solidness can likewise encourage and breathe life into communication — and make a name for an entrepreneur who is resolved to stick out.

5. Successful Business Communication Is Considerate

You definitely realize that successful business communication abilities rely upon you venturing into the shoes of the beneficiary with the goal that you can tailor your message appropriately. Thought ups the ante by infusing some enthusiastic knowledge all the while — by demonstrating enthusiasm, being certain and hopeful, maintaining a strategic distance from "you" for "we" and empowering questions. In any event, when your message doesn't incite a grin or gratefulness, your conveyance can.

6. Successful Business Communication Is Correct

It ought to abandon the saying that business communication ought to be right, if not faultless. Be that as it may, in this time of "hustle just a bit" communication, who hasn't seen terrible messaging propensities, for example, ungrammatical or foolish shortened forms downer into different types of composed communication? Trust it: People will pass judgment on you – and your private company – by the words you use and how you use them. Appropriate spelling and accentuation are as indispensable as reports that are syntactically right.

7. Powerful Business Communication Is Courteous

Kindness is the last cousin in the horde of the seven C's of communication – and is firmly identified with thought yet is different enough to justify a different notice. Considerate communication is courteous and deferential communication – pervaded with such words and expressions as "Thank you" and "Please" and - in the verbal communication – direct eye-to-eye connection and the infrequent gesture of the head. Graciousness is likewise intelligent in nature - particularly verbal communication - as the beneficiary surveys your reaction.

If you're beginning to respect the seven C's of communication as a communication mixed drink, you can be guaranteed that you have the correct fixings – to achieve *effective business communication* as well as to cleanse those infrequent cerebrum issues.

TIPS FOR IMPROVING YOUR BUSINESS COMMUNICATION SKILLS

You realize that great communication abilities are basic to ascend to the top in business. Communications abilities can charm you among your companions, raise your incentive among your bosses, and cause you to be respected among those subordinate to you. Things being what they are, how might you create them to meet your actual potential? Here are some useful hints for improving your business communication abilities.

1. Practice Your Listening Skills (and Your Paying Attention Skills Too)

At the point when others are talking, would you say you are genuinely tuning in? We often befuddle 'tuning in' with 'being peaceful'; however, because you aren't talking while others are talking doesn't mean you're truly tuning in. Figure out your own interior discourse and genuinely tune into what others are stating. It often rehashes what you've heard with the goal that you realize you're focusing and they know it as well.

2. Team Up, Don't Dictate

Talks, monologs, and ramblings don't have a place in business communications. If you find you're talking in excess of a couple of minutes (with the exception of when giving an introduction or driving a show), stop. Simplify what you're attempting to state however much as could be expected. Enable others to offer their contribution to the issue. Communication is about giving and taking, not directing how things will be or how you figure they ought to be.

3. Focus on How You Spend Your Leisure Time

You presumably didn't anticipate that this should be on the rundown. What does the TV indicates you watch, the things you read, and your leisure activities have to do with business communications? All things considered, the appropriate response is twofold. To start with, they can possibly open you to new points of view and significant recent developments that help you develop your business insight. Chances are individuals who watch an hour of unscripted tv every day won't be as fit for conveying a business-situated discussion just as the individuals who invest their free energy perusing business diaries and systems administration with successful tutors.

Second, you will gather colossally valuable thoughts and bits of knowledge from more scholarly interests than from watching or perusing less supportive material during your off-time.

4. Put Resources into the Right Communication and Collaboration Tools

If you're relying upon email and internet-based life for your communications, you're likely getting a great deal of pointless and repetitive data and maybe passing up the most significant discussions. A collective apparatus like Vmoso is the perfect method to streamline communications, work together on significant activities, and assemble important business connections.

5. Try Not to Wait Too Long to Bring Up Sensitive Issues

Enabling a circumstance to construct and putrefy is a formula for a breakdown in communications. It's a lot simpler, more powerful, and increasingly professional to address an issue when it springs up, while it's still in its early stages, than to hold up until it develops into a major, monstrous, furious beast. More often than not, a brisk, direct talk can resolve any relational or professional issues without contrarily influencing the relationship.

6. Figure Out How to Have and Use a Good People Memory

Is Sheila a morning individual, or is it better to approach her with an issue later toward the evening? Does Samuel lean toward a bagel when you swing by to get breakfast, or would he say he is, to a greater degree, a frankfurter bread sort of fellow? Is it Tuesdays or Thursdays that Becky needs to leave at the earliest opportunity to get her kid to his orthodontist arrangement? Do these little subtleties appear to be inane to you? Individuals are significant. When you can recall insights regarding their own lives, it demonstrates that you care for them past their work. This cultivates a more profound, progressively significant relationship that will spill effectively into a superior, additionally remunerating business relationship.

WHY BETTER COMMUNICATION SKILLS LEAD TO MORE SALES SUCCESS

Figuring out how to impart all the more adequately with individuals who have diverse message styles than you do will lead you to more forecasts, increasingly beneficial discourses, and more deals.

Consider it. What is the essential reason for offers? Communication. Deals are at least two people speaking with one another, attempting to talk about what the issues are, and after that, examining potential answers for those issues from the dealer's side. Yet, here's the test. Most sales reps commit the error of portraying their items and administrations only from the position they're most acquainted with. They convey in a manner that has intuitively sounded good to them. They search inside for their communication model. I would recommend that you look remotely: that you identify what your prospect's message style is, and that you change your message style to coordinate the style of the individual you're cooperating with. Become familiar with this technique for communication here.

Prospects don't get paid to change the manner in which they purchase. Despite what might be expected, they're probably going to remain with the procedure that is as of now natural to them! In this manner, it's our duty as salesmen to impart such that will make it simpler for a purchaser to "incline toward" our discussion, to float towards us rapidly. That is really what we get paid to do!

For what reason is this significant? All things considered, accept I am the purchaser and accept that I'm a great "enormous picture" individual. I convey as far as. What's more, accept you, the vender, is a great "meticulous" communicator. Except you turn out to meet with me just because, and you hung out portraying the majority of the subtleties of how your item functions, separating every one of the specifications and giving me all the details. How likely would you be to associate with me on an individual level?

Not likely by any means. I think there would be a distinction. What's more, the genuine disaster would be me as a purchaser saying "no" to you, not because of your item, but since we didn't associate.

The vast majority will normally associate with about 18% to 20% of the populace. Learn to expect the unexpected. That leaves 80% of the populace that we as salesmen need to change our communication style for if we need to ensure that we coordinate! If we're not discussing appropriately with 80% of the populace, we can't hope to be focused on our business job by envisioning that 100% of the 20% we interface with normally will need to purchase.

How would we start? By focusing on our own communication style. We truly need to see how we speak with the world intuitively – who we bond with effectively. When we're mindful of that, progression number two is to have the option to identify the social attributes that our prospect is showing and react fittingly to them.

Actually, everybody is sending us a flag about how they like to convey, constantly. It's simply an issue of our figuring out how to tune in.

Individuals surrounding us are letting us know always, with their words and their activities, that they're intrigued speaking with us about the master plan, or about social connections, or about getting the raw numbers right, or about being a piece of a gathering. Our main responsibility is to figure out how to get on those signs they're sending and to react such that makes the individual-to-individual association almost certain with that specific person. As any individual who has invested any energy child-rearing can verify, there is nobody size-fits-all model when it comes to compelling communication. The main concern is: adaptability works. There are many ways that we at Sandler show you how to identify and react deftly and successfully to different communication styles:

Great communication Is significant in Deals with Success.

Sounds self-evident, isn't that so? You can't make a deal except if you've exhibited an incentive to a prospect. You can't do that except you've comprehended their issues and concocted a methodology to unravel them. Thus, you can't do that until you get your prospect to disclose to you what's up, etc.

What Is the Importance of Communication in Sales?

The foundation of offers' success is the capacity to assemble and give data such that makes your prospect need to work with you. Your offer, your estimating, even your item's highlights - none of that issues except if you're ready to get your prospects to converse with you and furthermore tune in to what you need to state.

That implies you must be amazingly sensitive to your purchaser and comprehend what they mean when they let you know - or don't let you know - something. It additionally implies that you can't simply roll out a rundown of advantages or motivations to cooperate. You must see how your prospects realize what they care about, what communication style they like, and adjust your system as needs are.

So, before you submerge yourself in purchaser personas, contextual analyses, and marketing security, take a shot at these aptitudes to guarantee that when you're conversing with a prospect, you're sending the correct message.

Crucial Communication Skills for Salespeople to Have

1. Give full consideration

We're all busier than at any other time, and selling can be a particularly weight-filled vocation. So it's reasonable that during a customer meeting, your brain could meander over to the demo you need to plan for this evening, the prospecting you neglected to do, or the agreement you're looking out for to come in.

Because it's justifiable doesn't make it satisfactory. Appearing at a call isn't just about physically being on the opposite stopping point. You need to commit 100% of your regard for each call, else you'll miss subtleties and make your prospect rehash things they've just let you know. It'll be evident when you're not focusing, and that is no real way to treat purchasers.

2. Practice undivided attention

In addition to the fact that you have to tune in, you need to listen effectively, or your discussion won't generally go anyplace.

"Time after time, sales reps are trusting that their turn will discussion or considering what to state straight away, rather than genuinely tuning in to the prospect," Databox CEO Peter Caputa says.

Caputa utilizes the accompanying four-advance procedure:

- Really tune in to the prospect.
- Input the substance and sentiment of the prospect's words.
- Affirm you heard the prospect accurately.

- Ask an applicable follow-up inquiry to further clarify your comprehension of their circumstance.

3. Peruse non-verbal communication and control your own

A similar sentence said by somebody who's grinning, looking straightforwardly at you, and sitting upright is gotten differently when the speaker is turning away and slumping - regardless of whether they implied something very similar the multiple times.

That is because while we can say practically anything we need, our non-verbal communication often uncovers our actual aims or importance. Incredible communicators realize how to peruse others' non-verbal communication so they can envision the course a discussion's going, and furthermore ensure their very own non-verbal communication isn't conveying signals they don't intend to communicate.

4. Ace the subtleties of voice tone

Like non-verbal communication, voice tone - your voice pitch, volume, speed, and even your assertion decision - influences how the words you're really saying are deciphered. What's more, if you're in inside deals, the main thing you need to establish a connection is your voice.

Tune in to how your prospect talks, then mirror their talking designs when it bodes well. While you most likely shouldn't mirror each slang word or language they use, slow down if they talk gradually - or speed things up if they talk quickly. Match your degree of custom and commonality to your prospect also. The key is to meet purchasers on their turf - and that implies talking in a manner they're alright with.

5. Be compassionate

You don't really need to concur with everything your prospect is stating, however you ought to consistently, in any event, attempt to see things from their perspective. What's more, that implies something other than saying, "Gee, I see where no doubt about it."

The best salespeople can associate with their prospects because they really comprehend the things their purchasers do at work each day and the difficulties they face. Not exclusively does being sympathetic make you increasingly amiable, it likewise expands your odds of getting it done. When you can draw on your insight into your prospects' genuine every day, you're better prepared to comprehend what they care about, which makes it more probable you'll have the option to support them.

6. Comprehend what's not being said

Prospects once in a while don't tell every bit of relevant information. What's more, that is alright, as long as you probably are aware of how to spot when it's occurring. Is your prospect simply assessing your organization because his supervisor guided him to show three choices? Is your prospect sold, however her chief, the monetary purchaser, isn't? These are essential things to know, and you can't suss them out until you figure out how to figure out the real story.

7. Talk in specifics

Extraordinary communicators aren't enticing because they talk in sensational, clearing talk. They're ready to persuade individuals because they can point to specific models or stories that help the fact of the matter they're attempting to make - and on account of salesmen, because they can show precisely how an item or highlight will support their purchaser.

Be as specific as possible. Also, if you can toss in an appealing soundbite or two, by all methods do it. Simply don't depend on quippy expressions to get it to the end goal.

8. Be a topic master

Obviously, you can't be specific if you don't have any thoughts about what you're discussing. If you offer to a specific industry, you should realize that business' worries, practices, and purchasing behaviors under control. If you offer to different enterprises, realize your worth prop as it identifies with every cold and uses client references as reinforcement.

Prospects will never believe you if it doesn't appear as though you truly comprehend your (or their) business, so become a specialist in your important field.

9. Realize what you don't have a clue

In any case, being a specialist doesn't mean you know it all. Except if you've shadowed your purchaser, you don't know precisely what they do or each subtlety of their business. So don't act as you do. You should realize enough to portray out the layouts of their circumstance all alone, however you'll generally need to depend on your prospects to fill in the little subtleties.

Know about the holes in your insight, then request that your prospect help fill them in. They'll value your genuineness about what you don't have the foggiest idea, and you'll abstain from losing bargains because of false suspicions.

10. Be truly inquisitive

The way to deals is posing great inquiries. Also, if you're not really inquisitive about your prospect's circumstance, it'll be very simple to slip into your lift pitch before you've set up whether any piece of it is significant to your purchaser. Extraordinary communicators are normally inquisitive about their conversational partners, and that is particularly pivotal in deals - pose inquiries first, then answer them later.

11. Accept great aim

In some cases, prospects forget about significant arrangements that can change the direction of an arrangement. Now and then, they make a responsibility before they've gotten an endorsement from the important partners. In some cases, they lie intentionally. The majority of the above circumstances are baffling - and some positively cause for irritation. Be that as it may, it's often difficult to recognize circumstances where a purchaser misdirected you intentionally and one where they made a veritable blunder.

Forming a hasty opinion about your prospect's goal will shade the remainder of your associations in a negative light. Continuously expect great aim so you're not intuitively treating your prospects with the antagonistic vibe.

12. Continuously be straightforward

Because you're accepting great expectation doesn't mean your prospect will, so consistently be forthright about the inquiries you can reply, the inquiries you can't, and the inquiries with answers your prospect may not really like.

Your prospects won't be straightforward about their objectives and zones for development except if they trust you. That implies continually being forthright when you don't know something so they accept what you're stating when you do know the appropriate response.

13. Try not to make presumptions

if you've been in similar deals work for some time, you can without much of a stretch fall into everyday practice. Yet, because the initial 100 prospects that fit a specific profile had similar issues and procedures doesn't mean the 101st will.

Except if you have freely verified a snippet of data or your prospect has said the words to you, never make a suspicion about their circumstance. While it just takes a couple of moments to ask a subsequent inquiry, making a prospect feel overlooked and compelling them to intrude on you to address a supposition, that is a negative gradually expanding influence that can keep going forever.

14. Be persevering, not irritating

There's a scarcely discernible difference among perseverance and bugging, and it's significant for sales reps to get it. Proceeding to call and email your prospect without realizing for what reason they're not reacting is counterproductive and can just serve to bother and estrange them.

If you haven't got a reaction to a subsequent message, attempt a different methodology. Rather than sending a similar email to your prospect, start crisp with another feature and a simpler source of inspiration. When you reconnect them, steer the discussion back to business.

15. Be OK with quietness

Deals veteran Jeff Hoffman says most sales reps are excessively awkward with quietness. When they pose an inquiry and the prospect gets calm, most reps quickly attempt to fill that quiet by asking a subsequent inquiry or clarifying their inquire.

Hoffman prescribes delaying for around three-to-five seconds before talking. That way, you're not interfering with a significant idea your prospect may have, and you're starting the trend that quietness is welcome in your discussions.

APPROACHES TO BUILD CONSUMER TRUST NATURALLY

Before clients make a buy from you, they should have the option to confide in you. They have to believe that your messages are exact; that what you're selling matches up to what you state it is and that if anything turns out badly with the exchange, you'll bolster them.

The issue is, trust can't be set up rapidly or through tricks; organizations that have lost buyer trust know this very well. As they attempt to fix their picture, they understand that a bunch of promotions can't fix the adverse relationship in individuals' psyches. Trust can't be constrained down individuals' throats, and it can't be deceived out of individuals.

Rather, you need to acquire customers' trust normally. In any case, how might you do this?

1. Improve your security.

Initially, ensure your clients have a sense of security when they shop with you. Regardless of whether you aren't selling your items through a web-based business stage, clients will in any case be visiting your site, and the measure of security they feel while there can assume a significant job in the amount they trust your image.

For instance, if you spam them with publicizing or keep up a checkout procedure that is cumbersome and difficult to pursue, clients may speculate that your foundation is perilous. In this way, hamburger up your security with essential SSL assurance; utilize trusted installment choices, and show your trust identifications gladly - trust seals are the single most prominent on-location factor that builds customer trust.

2. Be socially dynamic (and obvious).

Being dynamic via web-based networking media encourages you in various manners: You manufacture perceivability for your image, you pull in more adherents and you find that the devotees you do draw in have a superior vibe for "who" your image is. The more, as often as possible, you uncover this side of your image, the quicker you'll have the option to manufacture that trust.

One of the qualities of structure perceivability by means of web-based social networking is the measure of adaptability you have there: You can invest your energy syndicating nearby substance, drawing in with new and past adherents, posting pictures and video or refreshing clients with news and data. The key is to be dynamic and present on a social stage.

3. Under-guarantee and over-convey.

Purchasers don't confide in brands so much as they used to, and one purpose behind this shift is that clients feel they've been deceived. Whenever a client feels just as the person in question has been misled or controlled, in any way that client will probably go separate ways with the brand dependable.

Appropriately, it's to your greatest advantage to under-guarantee and over-convey when it goes to all types of client desires. If it takes you seven days to send an item, tell your clients it takes two weeks. If an item will keep going for a long time, guarantee it will keep going for eight. That way, you'll never risk breaking your guarantees (in any event, not with most of your clients).

4. Go hard and fast for client support.

Trust ends up delicate when clients have an issue with something. If they experience an issue and get quick, accommodating and significant client assistance, they'll consider you perpetually as a dependable brand.

Be that as it may, if you fail, you'll lose a client perpetually and likely experience a plunge in your notoriety. Whenever you can, go full scale in your client care. Don't simply go to the most cost-productive approach to determine an issue; ensure your clients feel heard and acknowledged, and make a special effort to satisfy them.

5. Make your image progressively close to home.

It additionally makes your image progressively close to home, in your promoting and publicizing, just as in your customary associations with clients and customers. Try not to utilize contents and conventional reactions; rather, urge your workers to talk from the heart, and connect with clients like genuine individuals.

This little change causes your image to appear to be more human than corporate, and can radically change clients' impressions of you to improve things.

6. Impart more.

Absolutely never leave your clients in obscurity. In spite of the fact that there is such an incredible concept as over-communication, when in doubt, the more you converse with your clients, the better. This is particularly valid if you're working with customers one-on-one, state, as a specialist or an advertiser.

Be open and straightforward about your objectives and forms, and if something ever turns out badly, recognize the blunder proactively. If you've discovered retention subtleties or ignoring the informative side of the relationship, any trust you may have assembled could self-destruct.

7. Continuously be accessible.

Along those equivalent lines, it's imperative that your image consistently be accessible, here and there, for the individuals who need it. On presentation pages, including a telephone number or a moment visit box can right away build your change rate. Why? Because individuals feel ameliorated realizing they can chat with somebody whenever they pick.

Ensure your clients have various lines of contact for you consistently - and if you have a devoted record agent, give your customers that individual's phone number if there should be an occurrence of a crisis.

Building trust won't come rapidly, and won't generally be clear, however these seven methodologies can get you headed the correct way. From that point, your most dominant system will be consistency. The more reliable you are with your image character, your client support and your fundamental items and administrations, the more faithful your current clients will be and the more grounded your notoriety will develop.

Tragically, even the best client trust systems require time and tolerance to develop. Along these lines, start now.

Business communication has substantially more significance than numerous individuals figure it out. Truth be told, an examination by the Project Management Institute found that poor communication was the explanation for the disappointment of 33% of all bombed tasks it studied.

Nothing unexpected then that communications can have an effect on whether your business wins the certainty and fulfillment of your customers. You need to realize how to converse with them and give them the positive impression that spots you over the challenge.

Need to wow your customers? Then set aside the effort to fundamentally look at your communications technique and apply these four critical tips.

1. Give extremely quick reactions.

To give an excellent encounter to your customers - including the individuals who are entrepreneurs - your convenient reaction can best the entirety of your other client support endeavors. Most business proprietors comprehend that maintaining a business requires hours past the customary 9 to 5. Along these lines, your reactions to requests and messages shouldn't be bound to the run of the mill workday, if you need to address clients' issues.

As a business person, you'll be occupied and inaccessible at specific occasions, yet this doesn't pardon your disregarding demands. Just addressing inquiries, or telling somebody that you will react when you can, can have a significant effect. Sending reactions to customers at night or on an end of the week will demonstrate that you are happy to go the additional mile.

Be certain that your reactions are expeditious as well as clear and brief. Numerous business proprietors battle with straightforward email behavior and tend to over-clarify (or under-clarify) certain ideas. This can cause disarray, and now and again dissatisfaction. Utilizing an altering system like MailMentor can enable you to provide better answers by estimating the perusing difficulty of what you compose, and featuring vague sentences.

2. Never under-gauge the estimation of casual conversation.

By the day's end, customers work with individuals, not organizations. Along these lines, building affinity with them is fundamental for making long haul business connections and better brand trust. The key here is making your business amiable, to assemble an association.

View this systems' administration open door as an approach to become acquainted with your customers as individuals, not simply clients. Set aside the effort to visit with your customers as you would with companions or associates. Following up after an underlying gathering or telephone call demonstrates that you are eager to make a special effort to give an excellent, acculturated business experience.

3. Utilize a tried and true inside framework.

Potential and existing customers need to feel certain about their decision to banding together with you. Illuminating them about the frameworks your business places into training can ease any worry they may have. Customers need to see that you are reliable and that the little subtleties of their undertakings don't risk escaping everyone's notice. Consequently, spreading out your arrangement for how you will proficiently create top-notch work, all the way, is an astute move.

If you haven't as of now, executing a dependable undertaking, the executives and joint effort framework can truly help your business when it comes to communication and profitability. Given all the software arrangements now available, finding the ideal one to meet your requirements will probably require some exploration.

For example, Nutcache is a task-the-board instrument that allows you to actualize and pursue coordinated procedures and techniques; an enormous pattern among present-day new companies. Nutcache plans to simplify cooperation and coordinated effort by giving viable communication devices that keep everybody on the up and up. The subsequent straightforwardness and clearness will facilitate customers' stresses.

Discussing the procedures your organization pursues is an extraordinary method to win customers' trust in your business' capacity to convey. Reveal to them how often your colleagues meet, what your everyday timetable resembles during a venture and how every part adds to creating the best outcomes.

4. Converse with clients as you would to your chief.

Customers are the ones with the checkbook. Along these lines, basically, they are your chief. While they come to you for your skill, at last, they are the ones making major decisions.

Before you plunge into a venture, set aside the effort to examine their ideal results and clear up any perplexity or potential barriers. Once more, this boils down to clear and open communication with your customers.

Try not to accept the subsequent stage, and consistently run any progressions by the customer first.

When you prescribe approaches to achieve their objectives, don't talk in absolutes ("We can't do this"; "You should purchase this program"). Rather, express your thoughts as proposals while delineating the stars, cons and hazard factors. Solicit them what they anticipate from you, however don't overpromise anything you can't convey on.

Great businesses know the significance of sound customer connections. Monetarily, it costs four to multiple times less to keep a customer than to gain another one.

So as to assemble these kinds of faithful clients, you should build up trust and certainty through appropriate communication. A little exertion goes far, so contribute an opportunity to become acquainted with your customers and learn successful techniques for certain and commonly useful talk.

Communication Tips That Will Boost Customer Trust

If you need the most faithful clients- ones that will stay with you for quite a while - you have to fabricate client trust. Probably the ideal approach to fabricate client trust is by giving incredible client care. When your clients realize that you have their backs, they'll have total trust in you as an organization.

In addition, extraordinary client assistance can even build deals. As indicated by insights from American Express, 7 out of 10 U.S. purchasers state they've spent more cash to work with an organization that conveys extraordinary help.

Yet, incredible client support isn't just about taking care of the issues of your clients. To convey prevalent client assistance, you have to step up your communication abilities.

Look at these 5 communication tips that will support client trust:

1. Be straightforward.

The initial step to improve your communication with clients is to be straightforward. Straightforwardness is presently the new ordinary in business. Being straightforward implies that, as a business proprietor, you have to stay open with your clients in regards to your business objectives, history, execution, tasks, etc. In any event, during a brand emergency, you can keep up client trust by being straightforward. Truth be told, as indicated by measurements, 85% of individuals are bound to stay by a business during a brand emergency if it has a background marked by being straightforward.

In this way, endeavor to be transparent with your clients. Besides offering data to your clients, get input from your clients too. Approaching your clients for their conclusion in a client criticism review will give you incredible bits of knowledge and make them feel esteemed. Simply remember to tell your clients that you're anticipating utilizing the information they give to all the more likely to serve them.

2. Become more acquainted with your clients.

When giving client assistance, you ordinarily are most worried about getting to the base of the issue and fathoming it in a convenient way. Be that as it may, don't think little of the intensity of the casual discussion. Conversing with your clients like they're your companions is a compelling method to support clients' trust and makes certain to intrigue them. Your clients will recollect that you set aside the effort to get some information about themselves.

Along these lines, make certain to invest energy to ask your clients how their days are going, what their objectives are in utilizing your item/administration, and follow up after beginning discussions to perceive how they're doing. Becoming more acquainted with your clients will enable them to see the individuals behind the brand.

3. Offer various communication channels.

Because of innovation today, individuals have a huge amount of choices. While a few people still incline toward the good old telephone call, different clients lean toward utilizing different stations to get their client care questions replied. In this way, it's significant that you offer various communication channels to your clients.

For example, web-based life is getting to be one of the most well-known channels for clients to air their grievances. Investigate how JetBlue Airways handles upset clients on Twitter.

Giving different roads for client assistance; for example, telephone, email, content informing, and online life will expand trust because your clients realize that they'll have the option to get a grip of you a wide range of ways. Additionally, you'll have the option to take into account every one of your clients' novel needs and inclinations.

4. Be brisk with your reactions.

Only a couple of years back, if you had a client support issue you'd need to contact the business on Monday-Friday between 9am-5pm, and once in a while sit tight hours or days for a reaction — however no more. Clients today are accustomed to getting a practically prompt answer. Actually, as indicated by Small Business Trends, 82% of purchasers anticipate prompt reaction on deals or advertising questions. In this way, you should be extremely quick when reacting to client care issues.

Giving speedy reactions demonstrates to your clients that they're your top need. When a client realizes that they can get a prompt reaction, they'll believe that you'll generally be there to support them. This isn't useful for holding clients, however clients who haven't made a buy yet won't be as reluctant to do so because you can move their worries immediately.

5. Add live talk to your site.

Talking about extremely quick reactions, one of the most famous and must-have client care channels today is live visit. Clients need to realize that you'll be there for them whenever they have an issue, which is the reason for adding a live talk to your site. It is an incredible method to lift trust with clients.

With the live visits on your site, you can give helpful client support as well as guide clients through all phases of the purchaser's adventure.

Besides, regardless of whether you can't be there for your clients day in and day out, you can utilize a chatbot WordPress module or redistribute your live visit so your clients can find solutions at whenever. Truth be told, as indicated by LTVplus, live visit redistributing is demonstrated to expand e-Commerce transformation rates by 11X.

Over to you.

Communication is the way to stunning client care. When you improve communication with your clients, you can expand trust, make lifelong fans, and even create more deals. In this way, open the lines of communication with your clients and let them realize that you're there for them — consistently.

POWERFUL BUSINESS COMMUNICATION TECHNIQUES

With the ascent in innovation and business getting globalized, even the methods for successful business communication are evolving. With the development and ascent of your business, you will surely require viable, just as useful, methods of business communication in your working environment.

Indeed, even the exploration shows that the business associations' method for dealing with worker communication is changing indispensably to make business communication compelling in the work environment.

In an examination done by Towers Watson in 2012, it has been discovered that the organizations advancing viable business communication procedures are every now and again utilizing one-on-one dialogs alongside intelligent media so as to remain associated with their group.

Such associations are seen as higher-performing firms because of powerful business communication. Considering the significance of powerful business communication, we have thought of the best thoughts that advance it. We should look at them:

Successful Business Communication:

First Idea: Important Business Communications can be imagined

We should discover which works best - telling or demonstrating to somebody how the things should be finished?

For sure the appropriate response will appear, because visual learning is a useful method of business communication. In the event that organizations need to move bunches of data, some of it will be lost once the business communication procedure is finished.

To make the "clingy impact" on the collectors' psyche, be it for client socioeconomics or deals cycles, the group won't go through all the data in content pages. Then again, visuals will absolutely help in comprehending each and every thing the group needs to guzzle.

Make infographics, which are a straightforward yet appealing instrument of showing the data in a wonderful and satisfactory way. These can be effectively made by utilizing instruments like outwardly and Infogram.

Infographics are proficient styles of making statistical data points effectively absorbable just as can be effectively alluded back as well.

Model Warby Parker utilizes infographics as visuals so as to recap the whole year for their group. Warby Parker, an expert in glass edge structures makes its yearly report utilizing a visual substance, portraying significant achievements of the year.

Criticism is not constantly negative, rather positive inputs consistently center around making enhancements and help in creating trust and shared collaboration. Both workers just as a manager can improve their method for working by utilizing useful feedback.

By being available to criticism, the organization depicts a picture of being available to productive analysis, while inviting contribution from everybody in the organization.

This unquestionably helps in improving the work environment productivity as everybody will improve the way. What is the ideal approach to get feedbacks?

The review is the easiest method to gather information or input of the staff on everything from work culture to a representative new procuring procedure or employment fulfillment.

A portion of the outstanding study apparatuses are SurveyMonkey (helps in sending overviews) and 15 Five which simply needs a short way for the representatives to rapidly answer to few inquiries consistently.

So as to make the reactions increasingly fair and to get basic reactions, the colleagues ought to be permitted to react without unveiling their personality.

Model: ING Direct Canada enables its representatives by furnishing them with no activity titles just as no offices.

In this manner, anybody is permitted to chat with anybody and pioneers consistently attempt to evacuate the hindrances by respecting any sort of criticism or contributions from their group.

The inputs can be sure or negative and the representatives are never policed in regards to community condition in which they work.

A considerable lot of us get befuddled between tuning in and focusing. Therefore the majority of the representatives neglect this simple and basic hint for powerful business communication.

While talking or connecting with somebody, don't simply tune in to whatever they are stating rather be mindful and give careful consideration.

If you get an email with respect to any issue in the group, don't overlook it. Take a stab at looking for the issue of the significant subtleties covered up in the message sent.

If one of the colleagues is airing some sort of complaint, listen attentively, ensure you focus on the issue.

"If you can't clarify it basically, you don't comprehend it all around ok."

- Albert Einstein

Clearness is the most significant piece of compelling business communication. While composing or talking, one ought to be clear about what one needs to pass on. For the most part the gatherings are short and time-bound, so it is better that you ought to create clearness about what you talk and need to clarify.

Certainty is another significant component which should be clubbed with lucidity. The greater part of the compelling open speakers depicts conviction through their style of talking.

This is the ideal method for keeping individuals occupied with the discussion. This connecting with procedure requires self-assurance alongside better business communication aptitudes.

You ought to exhibit an eagerness to impart skill just as learning to the colleagues; this will unquestionably advance lucidity and certainty inside work culture.

Culture is the individuals whom the association enlists and the manner in which the individuals are overseen in the association or the way wherein the colleagues impart.

Along these lines, any association that advances sound culture will effectively impart the way of life to the group. Strengthening a positive and strong culture will build up a reasonable comprehension between workers.

By basically surrounding the practices alongside authoritative qualities in composed structure, the firm can without much of a stretch advance the way of life inside groups. Along these lines the group will viably pursue its pioneers, while placing these practices enthusiastically.

One of the powerful methods for conveying an organization's way of life is by taking the assistance of the culture deck. Culture Decks are a sort of visuals made by associations that can be counseled later on too by the representatives.

The innovative part of culture decks makes them simple to peruse just as very pleasant stuff.

A portion of the incredible highlights a culture deck ought to incorporate are:

- How crucial the association is
- Sort of individuals selected and procured in association
- Organization esteems in detail
- The devices just as styles of business communication being utilized
- Difficulties looked by the organization
- Overseeing styles and desires for representatives

For instance Netflix uses culture decks that were a moment hit in the business area as they were engaging, authentic, straightforward, clear just as groundbreaking.

The straightforwardness that appeared in the way of life decks helped in strengthening the association's validity and depicted Netflix as an incredible work environment.

The bigger the size of the association, the more difficult it is to pass on the message to every single representative of the association. To handle this issue of business communication inside associations, successful strategies or modes should be created.

The messages are not perused normally by the staff; the majority of the staff totally disregards the intranet messages. It is only the kitchen babbles that movements are quick and arrives at everybody in the organization.

An extremely successful method for speaking with the whole group inside stipulated time is to post the news or the updates normally on the office shows. With innovation close by you can put TV screens to the best use by sharing updates that are identified with:

- Organization's landing page or blog
- Up and coming occasions or gatherings
- Most loved News channels

- Photographs the items alongside the group pictures
- Deals Metrics and KPIs
- New position openings
- New Recruitments or advancements in association
- Limited time crusades or recordings
- Prizes and Recognitions

Like ESPN, the Wall Street Journal and so forth continue illuminating the workers about the most recent related accounts of the business or about the well-known outlets. This will absolutely keep the group refreshed about the most recent news that is applicable to them.

What is the new item on the square and when is the dispatch date? What might be the sticker price for the new item? What is the deadline to do the rebranding dispatch for the item?

It scarcely matters what is being sold by the organization, what is significant is that every one of the representatives and administrators ought to be in agreement in connection to the most recent advancement in the association.

For this situation to illuminate all the colleagues or the workers of the organization about the present position task or item guide is the best device.

A guide, much the same as infographics is an extremely convenient visual instrument that causes the representatives to know in detail what is as yet expected of them before anything new is to be propelled.

A portion of the distinctive highlights of a guide include:

- The item vision
- Point by point item includes
- Measurements and KPIs

- Courses of events and Milestones

A guide is a compelling device that relevantly portrays every single colleague's job alongside the ultimate objective. It additionally builds up a structure that encourages each colleague to anticipate a successful future for their item.

You can utilize an extremely successful and helpful instrument that helps with making guides and that is called Aha! It is an extremely helpful device that can likewise be refreshed alongside the advancement made by the organization.

Everybody in this world needs to be a pioneer and doesn't prefer to be controlled or oversaw. A similar hypothesis applies if there should arise an occurrence of associations too. So quit micromanaging, by giving the groups the opportunity and making them responsible for their work.

Each worker just needs that their work is finished. Being a decent administrator, you should quit keeping a tab on the worker over and over. Or maybe give them the freedom to check in toward the finish of either consistently or before the week's over.

This should be possible effectively either through every day/week by week updates messages, short quick-fire gatherings or slacks directed normally. Self-detailing will make them answerable for their work without having the sentiment of being controlled. This will positively help in advancing successful business communications as done by Shopify that uses an apparatus called iDoneThis, for sending ordinary updates as an email to the groups.

H.O.T approach can be explained as:

H - Honest

O - Open

T - Two-way

This is an exceptionally compelling methodology from advancing successful and positive business communication in associations. A large portion of the successful associations today executes HOT methodology to keep up higher business communication principles and to get alluring outcomes moreover.

A portion of the essential things of this procedure are:

- Continuously pursue the way of truth-telling false data or uncovering the realities. This will prompt most noticeably awful circumstances if discovered.

- Continuously be open as this will help in advancing receptiveness inside the colleagues.

- Continuously embrace two-path communication by being open to the perspective of others so as to build up better business communication, while giving others likewise to talk.

The formula of making a contention is straightforward. Simply place a couple of individuals in a typical space for 7 hours consistently, and 5 days in seven days. It is without a doubt that following a week or so strife would be made even in a scholarly and good group. Before the contentions ruin the communication between the group, it attempts to halt it from developing in any way.

Simply tell the representatives that the entryway of the room is constantly open, advance straightforwardness and request that they connect with the chief whenever any contention or issue emerges in the organization.

Make a legit and agreeable condition round you, where they feel great in coming to you and voicing the genuine concerns. It's the chief's obligation to determine and discover the answer for the issues with a receptive outlook and without receiving a judgmental methodology.

Conveying the organization's objectives to the workers and asking them the right inquiries and mindfully tuning in to their reactions will help in settling the debates in a compelling way.

COMPELLING BUSINESS COMMUNICATION AND WHY IS IT IMPORTANT?

Did you know, not utilizing compelling business communication could be costing your organization cash?

Consistently, we get down to business without investing a lot of energy by the way we will speak with others, when we arrive, or how compelling it will be.

A large portion of us is totally negligent of the effect our communication aptitudes have on the success of our vocation, not to mention if it is stripping the organization of cash.

How we talk, compose, or tune in, could be influencing our activity execution, advancement status, or our odds of an increase in salary.

When communication is incapable, the capacity to arrange or arrive at a deal, changes. Once being assignments which could create potential leads and profits, all of a sudden transforms into an all-out exercise in futility.

Shockingly, figuring out how to execute viable business communication at work, doesn't ordinarily sit high on our need list.

Saying this doesn't imply that we are purposely attempting to impede our professional development, yet our obliviousness of the amount job communication plays in the positions we fill, could be doing what we dread most, keeping us from climbing in the organization.

Numerous representatives accept, since they "landed the position," or, have never been "addressed" about the manner in which they impart at work, they should do it right.

Playing a speculating game with occupation execution is certifiably not a sound vocation plan. Something must be finished.

The inspiration to improve our communication abilities, must originate from us, and ought not exclusively to be dependent on the input given, or deficiency in that department, by our supervisors and partners.

It is our obligation to find out about compelling business communication and why it is fundamental in the working environment, and we will. On the whole, we should quickly cover the different kinds of communication we normally use.

A BRIEF OVERVIEW OF THE DIFFERENT TYPES OF COMMUNICATION

The primary idea that flies into a large portion of our brains when we hear, "Communication," is that of an individual talking, yet there is substantially more to this word than basic, "babble."

There are three primary sorts of communication:

1. **Verbal Communication** – How we convey what needs to be, using words.

i.e., Sounds, Language, Writing, Announcements, Letters, Dialog, Monologs, and Speech.

2. **Non-Verbal Communication** – How we convey what needs to be, through activities.

i.e., Physical Touch, Facial Expressions, Listening, Gestures, Body Language, and Eye Contact.

3. **Visual Communication** - How we convey what needs to be, using visuals.

i.e., Advertising, Signs, Graphics, Films, Photographs, and Designs.

The outcomes from a communication study appeared, by and large, individuals spend around 70 to 80 percent of their days utilizing some type of communication.

Of that time, we commonly spend around 9 percent composing, 16 percent perusing, 30 percent talking, and 45 percent tuning in.

Quite a bit of what we do and say during our time addresses what our identity is, the means by which we feel, and think, in addition to other things. Regardless of whether it is purposeful or not, we are continually speaking with others, as they are to us.

For example, a basic yawn can suggest the individual is drained or exhausted, and a steady sniffle can impart to others that the individual may catch a virus.

Apply a similar plan to more business related communication styles, and all of a sudden it will all turn out to be clear. i.e., How you compose messages, tune in during gatherings, and lead introductions.

Think about the different ways you convey once a day and the messages they send — Do you often think about their adequacy?

As people, we can't go a waking minute without utilizing some verbal, non-verbal, or visual communication, and this statement by Mark Twain can undoubtedly be seen as a depiction of the different communication types, since it utilizes them to pass on its message.

"Words are just painted fire; a look is simply the fire."

WHAT IS EFFECTIVE BUSINESS COMMUNICATION AND WHY IS IT IMPORTANT?

Huge numbers of us go through eight hours or increasingly a day at work, which causes most of our everyday communication to occur during office hours.

Not knowing to what degree the communication we use at work is helping or impeding us, makes it considerably harder to measure how well we are getting along in accomplishing our objectives and the objectives of the business.

Comprehension and utilizing powerful communication, is basic to improving as a business and worker.

All in all, what is Effective Business Communication? It is the procedure of at least two individuals sharing data that sends a reasonable message, and it is gotten, as planned.

When it is utilized at work, this type of communication can significantly build the organization's success.

When we represent, with, or for the benefit of the business, the utilization of successful communication, makes work guidelines, assignments, data, desires, alongside work forms, better to get it.

Then again, if the manner in which we convey at work is incapable, which most are, the organization winds up paying for it, truly.

It might be difficult to accept, yet organizations with as meager as 100 representatives, spend, all things considered, around 17 hours seven days clarifying past communication, which, when converted into dollar signs, rises to roughly $525,000.

Knowing this is the aftereffect of incapable communication, and that it is preventable, resembles adding salt to an open injury.

An unequivocal eye-opener, business proprietors need to begin making a move by executing the utilization of successful business communication.

In making it a high need, organization proprietors can check for communication issues and attempt to improve them, by offering an assortment of arrangements in the working environment.

Adding helpful segments about communications to different organization structures and procedures, similar to representative onboarding, will show workers the estimation of communication from the beginning.

Supervisors can energize dialogs during occupation execution gatherings, just as, offer viable business communication preparing.

Some may think, "However this will cost the organization cash," in all actuality, you are losing cash by not doing it.

In any event, the cash you spend on offering things like helpful communication courses will be for the improvement of the business, not at all like the costs you are encountering now.

Something else, the pointless loss of cash will keep on happening, including the misuse of worker time and profitability, bringing about a consistent cycle of the loss of organization dollars.

The data we share in our everyday work messages, bulletins, telephone calls, and in gatherings, are right now not disarray free, nor simple to peruse, and these are just a portion of the principal reasons your organization is losing cash.

A large number of us "hit" the email send button, without the slightest hesitation, giving next to no consideration, if any whatsoever, to the adequacy of our communication and the messages we are sending.

Having to consistently rehash directions, necessities and venture goals, to workers or partners, is definitely not an appropriate method to maintain a business, yet, this is accurately what number of us are as of now working.

We keep on enabling poor communication to hurt our primary concern while limiting the organization's odds at success.

The lion's share of laborers need to convey genuine worth and be a supporter of more prominent benefit of the organization, causing it much harder to comprehend why we too acknowledge this training, yet sadly, we do.

It's a well-known fact that the success of an organization is an immediate impression of the individuals running it, which is the reason compelling business communication needs to turn into an indispensable piece of our workplaces.

Numbness can never again be the motivation behind why businesses keep on losing cash from incapable communication.

Revealing insight into the effect communication has on our work, ideally, will motivate others to make the following stride, which is to create reasonable business communication aptitudes.

When utilizing this type of communication, in addition to the fact that you are ready to interface better with others, increment your range, and complete more undertakings in any case, you are additionally ready to create more income for yourself and the organization.

STEP BY STEP INSTRUCTIONS TO DEVELOP EFFECTIVE BUSINESS COMMUNICATION SKILLS

One of your top professional objectives ought to be to cultivate your work connections through viable communication.

Going past employment-related exchanges, you ought to utilize it in all types of communication.

A scholarly range of abilities, successful business communication is something you should acclimate yourself with and figure out how to create.

Through training, your communication will strengthen, and its viability will move into the employments you do, attempting your work endeavors powerful as well.

One key segment expected to develop as a drawing in a worker is mindfulness.

Pay heed to ALL your day by day verbal, non-verbal, and visual communication propensities to end up deliberate with the words and activities you use at work.

When hoping to change, grow, and better yourself, improvement needs to happen.

Here are four different ways to help build up your business communication abilities to make them compelling.

Fulfillment —

- Ensure the communication you offer and convey to others is finished.

- Incorporate the majority of the realities required by the group of spectators.

- Be exact in the words you use to express your expected message.
- Shun making any suppositions about the collector.

Rightness –

- Twofold check your work to guarantee there are no punctuation or spelling blunders.
- If utilizing outlines, charts, or insights, to improve your communication, the data must be exact.
- Your communication should be intelligible.

Compactness –

- Make your message compact and not, "tedious."
- Utilize fewer words, to precisely pass on your message, without decreasing its essential importance.

Lucidity –

To guarantee your message is completely clear, it is prescribed to share just a single specific snippet of data one after another, to help decrease the open doors for perplexity.

Utilize fitting words - ones that best depict what you are endeavoring to state, share, ask, or demand.

As lucidity is a companion to communication, disarray is its adversary.

Representatives need to satisfy their assignments and complete ventures rapidly and proficiently, with as meager to and from communication as could be allowed.

The more clear the communication is, the simpler it will be to finish work undertakings accurately and on schedule.

Since picking up the learning that viable business communication is something other than words, rather, a blend of a few things, it is essential to recall and fuse them when building up your communication aptitudes.

For example, when composing, it is imperative to make sure to address the passage arrangement, style, and structure.

While talking, your manner of speaking, expressions in your discourse, and word decision, all affect the viability of your message.

When going past the "paper," there are different pieces of successful communication, which you should consider.

In getting to be aware of your motions, articulations, and non-verbal communication, it makes it simpler for others to "read" you, because, actually all that you do and say, matters.

It demonstrates, "How" we impart, is similarly as significant as "What" we convey. The accompanying statement is an ideal portrayal of this,

"I realize you think you comprehend what you thought I stated, however I don't know you understand that what you heard isn't what I signified" — Alan Greenspan

Because of the statement's sentence structure, from the start, the message is confounding and difficult to comprehend, which is the reason you undoubtedly needed to peruse it more than once.

Whenever in the uncertainty of what kind of communication to utilize, approach others for their supposition and direct your exploration utilizing the web.

Comprehending the stuff to strengthen your communication aptitudes will improve your work-life.

It will be simpler to achieve professional objectives by realizing how to adequately speak with your supervisors, chiefs, administrators, executives, and associates.

You will discover more entryways are opening up for you at work.

All of a sudden, you can turn into an incredible speaker, essayist, or moderator, and with customary practice, individuals will consider the activity you do.

Along these lines, the development in your communication aptitudes will prompt an expansion in your work environment esteem.

In the end, you will feel certain about your communication capacities that you will never again dread requesting an advancement, increase in salary, or the power-customer account you have been peering toward for a considerable length of time.

Powerful business communication will support you, your organization, and its workers, ascend the stepping stool of success, where you can progress to the exceptionally top and sparkle.

KEY STANDARDS OF BUSINESS COMMUNICATION

Each type of communication requires cooperating with someone else or gathering of individuals – your group of spectators.

It imagines correspondence as an exchange of messages between a sender and a gatherer through a medium or channel of correspondence. It begins a cycle of correspondence.

A message is encoded by the sender through sounds, formed words, pictures, video, imparted in language or non-verbal correspondence, for example flag, outward appearances and way of talking. The message then arrives at the collector – the group of spectators – who interprets it and may choose to react.

This transmission of messages isn't constantly direct, be that as it may. While the recipient hears or sees the message, a progression of issues going about as 'clamor', may restrict their ability to grasp or adjust it. These issues fuse the way wherein the message is discussed, issues with the development used, the collector's failure to process the message and an absence of shared conviction (for example social factors, such as qualities, convictions and language) among sender and collector. At times, when a typical foundation isn't shared, the individuals included need to make a solid effort to construct a common comprehension and, hence, trade a few messages or utilize a scope of different media.

The accompanying key standards of business communication will assist you with getting a message crosswise over to your collector. They are:

Comprehend your group of spectators

It is essential to comprehend and know about your group of spectators. They are the individuals you talk to and write to. You should tailor the substance and the method of communication to suit their highlights. These incorporate their inclinations and convictions, foundation, jobs and characters. Accepting that they will share your perspectives and your experience information may prompt mistaken assumptions; in this way it is essential to get ready altogether before speaking with individuals you have quite recently met and who might be from a different setting. This will push you to accomplish your present objective, yet in addition to manufacture or upgrade your business connections.

Make progress toward clearness

To be powerful, your message must be clear. Be that as it may, what is obvious to you (the sender) may not be to the collector, because of your different foundations. This is the reason for observing a standard method to compose a report, sort out a gathering or give an introduction, for instance, it can encourage communication. Observing standard linguistic guidelines and wording likewise delivers a message that is obvious to your group of spectators.

Comprehend the setting of your communication

When conveying for business purposes, you should know about the way of life of your association and that of every division or outside association with which you impart. Being aware of the more extensive multicultural setting of your group of spectators is basic as well. Without this understanding, you won't have the option to set up shared convictions and see one another.

Have an unmistakable reason as a top priority

The principle motivation to impart in a business setting is to accomplish a specific reason. Regardless of whether you need to just advise your crowd or approach inducing them, ensure you realize what you need them to comprehend and do. Think additionally about the relationship you have with your group of spectators and how you need this to create because of your communications. Now and again, building a decent long haul association with an associate or business accomplice might be your primary target. Whatever your motivation, if it is obvious to you, you'll have a superior possibility of making it unmistakable to them.

Select the most proper medium

Communication can happen through a scope of media, for example, gatherings, messages, telephone calls and reports. For this to be viable, you have to choose media that is fitting to your motivation and your specific situation.

In the accompanying advances, you will take a gander at these standards in detail and figure out how they can enable you to turn into a successful business communicator.

SALESFORCE ESSENTIALS, THE NEW WAY TO PRIVATE COMPANY GROWTH.

What does it take to maintain a successful business? A few people reveal to you it's the craft of identifying and taking advantage of a lucky break— the association of planning and karma. Some state arrangements and training best get ready individuals for the rigors of the business world. Still, others guarantee it's about associations. In any case, none of them offer the entire story.

There's one significant component that is basic: powerful communication. In reality, solid communication, more than some other factor, might be the main indicator of business success. Somehow or another, communication adds to every one of those different variables.

Communication causes us to find out about new chances, deal with our training, and at last keep up and develop significant associations. Be that as it may, it likewise helps inside a business; with representatives, clients, and investors, and in essentially every other part of the business.

In an economy where 80 percent of new businesses fizzle, each progression of the procedure tallies. Here are some key approaches to audit and improve your business communication and ensure you're taking advantage of it.

1. Give individuals what they need

This isn't tied in with advising individuals what they need to hear, however, that is a piece of the condition. Extremely, it's tied in with realizing how to converse with individuals. As it were, compose your communication so you uncover the data that is essential to your group of spectators first.

Normally capable speakers do this naturally. It bodes well to arrange a rundown with the most significant data toward the start, where it is destined to be taken note. Envision an altered pyramid: the key data is at the top (which puts forth your defense more grounded) with supporting data showed underneath. The craft of effectively measuring your crowd's needs and altering your discourse on the fly to more readily oblige it takes more nuance. Lawmakers on the battlefield face this test routinely. They never realize who will come to open occasions or what offhand addresses they'll get from residents and correspondents. Envision your client as a basic journalist: Make sure the majority of your communication underscores what they care about most.

2. Gain proficiency with some fast critical thinking procedures

You may think this abandons saying, yet it merits rehashing: Problem tackling is an essential piece of business.

These means may appear to be unessential until you experience an issue you don't have the foggiest idea how to fathom immediately. With a critical thinking convention built up, there is a system to respond to new issues. Regardless of whether an issue is totally new, a set request for activities can be concocted to rapidly seclude it. A convention causes you to remain dynamic and guarantees you have less personal time, in any event, when confronting a particularly dubious issue.

3. Utilize your habits

Individuals are brought up in an assortment of ways and are agreeable and awkward with different things. Notwithstanding our differences, we should all utilize great habits. In a book for Inc. Tim Askew expresses, "There is an explanation behind habits and affability and it isn't as a matter of common courtesy. The motivation behind habits is to give us a down to earth structure to manage one another... It is the paste of development and a utilitarian guide for managing in regular business."

Social graces are important in up close and personal communications and messages. Presently they likewise apply to client relations via web-based networking media, where expanded perceivability makes it even more imperative to react instantly and pleasantly to client concerns. Having great habits and social graces make each association, business or something else, smoother. Make a special effort to be considerate.

4. Practice enthusiastic insight

Enthusiastic insight is being in line with others' sentiments and feelings. It tends to be as basic as seeing and taking additional consideration when somebody is having an unpleasant week, or as intricate as understanding the authentic or social issues that may, by and by, influence somebody.

At work, high passionate knowledge guides social communications and enables individuals to cooperate all the more adequately. It improves communication and enables groups to prudently talk about differing feelings. Pioneers in an organization who effectively focus on others' feelings have more joyful workers because they are all the more socially mindful, are deferential of assorted variety, and expertise to deal with the struggle. This further means progressively positive connections with merchants and clients.

Particularly in our cutting edge world, where resistance and acknowledgment are required in great business conduct, it's imperative to consider chronicled and social settings with each move you make. Others will value your respect and compassionate cooperation with them.

5. Focus on nonverbal communication

Despite the fact that various examinations place the significance of nonverbal communication equivalent to or outperforming that of verbal communication, it keeps on being misjudged and disparaged. Businesspeople who have aced the capacity to convey nonverbally have a few unmistakable points of interest in the business circle, from radiating certainty to fortifying the position.

Outward appearances, pose, eye to eye connection, voice, and hand signals all fall into this class. Acing the specialty of nonverbal communication for business relations isn't simple, however can give another measurement in your communications with associates, just as companions.

6. In any case, don't depend on it

Nonverbal communication is best used to enhance your comprehension or experience of the association, not fill in for fundamental communication (particularly when examining significant issues). Hence, consistently decipher signals you see at a gathering. Try not to submit your general direction to one sign alone, but instead all in all, and for the general state of mind of the circumstance. Give extraordinary consideration to the nonverbal prompts numerous individuals pass up.

By a similar token, it's imperative to control the nonverbal signs you anticipate to your associates. Odds are you're giving endlessly pieces of information and additional data constantly, in any event, when you're not mindful of it. Gradually and cautiously think about how signals and articulations might be translated, both to enable you to get individuals, yet in addition to help individuals get you.

The primary concern: It's ideal to ace nonverbal communication before testing out motions and articulations that are outside of your customary range of familiarity during a significant gathering.

7. Be a genuine audience

It's out and out baffling when individuals profess to listen when they truly are simply trusting that their possibility will talk. An unfocused look, interferences, and listening just for the primary concern are for the most part poor listening propensities. Here's some unwelcome news: You most likely display poor tuning in every so often as well—and individuals see it.

This binds back to nonverbal communication. Such a large amount of the data we trade with other individuals isn't verbalized. If you figure out how to be a decent audience, universes will open up to you. Individuals love being tuned in to. It's most likely the simplest method to comfort somebody- Just tune in to what they need to state, and really be available for the discussion.

Incomprehensibly, managers particularly need to ace incredible listening aptitudes. Despite the fact that it's apparently the manager's business to guide individuals, if the supervisor needs to be valued and esteemed by their subordinates, the person will truly tune in to concerns and attempt to get it. It's this careful consideration that isolates great managers from extraordinary.

8. Challenge presumptions (graciously!)

Nobody likes pessimism, yet there are circumstances when the main proper activity is an exhaustive and point by point addressing the subject. It's human instinct to make suspicions—it spares us time each day—yet imagine a scenario in which you or another person lands at an inappropriate end. A few suppositions can be out and out risky to connections, business exchanges, or both, and you must question them when you see them.

We wouldn't fret perusers. As opposed to making suppositions regarding why a partner hasn't reacted to an email, if a customer is happy with your work, or if an inventive item will be profitable, pose inquiries. Focus on what matters you do know, and let the other individual fill in the rest. There are numerous instances of businesses passing up genuine open doors because they neglected to challenge their suspicions about new items or advancements until it was past the point of no return. Unobtrusively and deftly endeavor to comprehend the setting of the suspicion to check its worth. When you set aside the effort to challenge suppositions, you may adapt more data about the subject and improve your business accordingly.

9. Pose inquiries

This may appear to be like the past tip, yet it's really different. To some degree nonsensically, when you ask individuals inquiries in the social circle, getting data is really an optional objective. The objective is to get them to talk and unwind, and offer you the chance to rehearse those listening aptitudes. In business, the more data the better—however you have to pose the correct inquiries to gather that data.

Posing the correct inquiries requires exertion, however it can have monstrous prizes. If you realize the correct inquiries to pose, you can discover the data you need, and furthermore impart metadata about yourself. Posing shrewd inquiries is one approach to demonstrate your competency and ability over the topic, and is a basic piece of business organizing.

10. Be self-assured

In spite of the fact that a significant number of our tips have concentrated on being less decisive, it's difficult to be a decent pioneer without realizing when to put your foot down. When utilized wisely, being self-assured can have an extraordinary impact, one that is possibly upgraded when individuals know you as a touchy and obliging individual. This can show you're submitted when you truly need to. Being confident doesn't mean you need to be forceful or pushy, but instead clear and successful.

Truth be told, with a less confident administration style, it doesn't take a lot of solidness to get things going. Your workers will see your quality of direction and your drive to succeed and regard that. Give arranges prudently and individuals will pay heed.

Communication isolates a decent business from an extraordinary one

When you speak with individuals in your association all the more viably, you're increasingly mindful of potential issues and better ready to actualize arrangements. Concentrate on the abilities in this book to improve your communication in the work environment: You'll be increasingly educated about each part of the business and you'll comprehend the worries of your associates. If you speak with your clients well, you can get potential traps and different issues right off the bat. Evaluate the communication framework at your business and perceive how these tips work for you.

MAKE PROGRESS THROUGH EFFECTIVE BUSINESS COMMUNICATION

Making progress through viable business communication normally includes obtaining aptitudes and experience. Figure out how to express your thoughts plainly and compactly. Find a way to comprehend your group of spectators. Focus on your message to address their issues. Utilizing powerful communication enables your message to get translated effectively. Stay away from clashes with collaborators, administrators and clients by utilizing compelling communication techniques. Work on utilizing techniques, for example, undivided attention and summarizing to guarantee your success.

1. Dissect your group of spectators before you make an introduction or lead a gathering. Envision potential reasons for disarray and get ready clarifying articulations. As you get ready, attempt to see the circumstance from your group of spectators' viewpoint.

2. Give all the foundation important for individuals who get your email, introduction or talk to make a move, for example, settle on a choice dependent on the data you give. If your theme requires a far-reaching comprehension of complex basic ideas, state so from the get-go in your talk. Set clear assumptions regarding what you trust your business communication can accomplish.

3. Monitor the inquiries individuals pose to you and figure out how to react to the regular requests. Utilize undivided attention techniques, for example, rewording what you have heard or

gesturing in affirmation. Pose clarifying inquiries yourself to guarantee you really comprehend what your group of spectators doesn't grasp. Ask open-finished inquiries to begin a discussion, get more subtleties or get a contribution on issues. Pose shut inquiries that require a basic "yes" or "no" response to affirm your comprehension, get understanding or close a gathering.

4. Pick the correct communication design for every circumstance. For instance, abstain from utilizing email to impart intense subject matters, for example, awful news. Utilize composed communication to pass on arrangements of data, for example, approaches and methodology. Use outlines and diagrams to condense muddled money related information.

5. Proofread your composed communication, for example, email, reports or different records.

Check for spelling and language structure botches with the goal that you fix them before appropriating your data. For email messages, incorporate a powerful headline, talk about just a single subject and specify the sort of reaction you need.

6. Focus on non-verbal communication when conveying face to face. An individual who doesn't take a gander at you or seems occupied in different manners may not be capable to handle your message. Utilize physical prompts to tailor your message or know when it may be fitting to talk about the subject at some other point.

7. Concede judgment until the discussion closes. Abstain from intruding on the speaker with counter contentions. It confines your comprehension of the circumstance.

8. Perceive social differences in communication styles. Before you work with individuals from another nation, set aside the effort to examine business rehearses around there of the world.

Powerful Communication Means Business Success

The capacity to speak with individuals both inside and outside your association is a key normal for successful business manufacturers.

Powerful communication strengthens the associations between an organization and the majority of its partners and advantages businesses from numerous points of view: Stronger basic leadership and quicker critical thinking; prior notice of potential issues; expanded efficiency and steadier work process; more grounded business connections; more clear and progressively convincing advertising messages; improved professional pictures for the two managers and organizations; lower worker turnover and higher representative fulfillment; and better money related outcomes and better yield for financial specialists.

The requirement for communication aptitudes

The significance of communication isn't astounding when you consider the stunning measure of time individuals spend imparting at work. One examination, distributed in Business Outlook, in view of the reactions from more than 1000 managers at Fortune 1000 organizations found that laborers send and get a normal of 1798 messages every day through phone, email, faxes, papers, and up close and personal communications. A few specialists have assessed that the normal business official spends roughly 75% to 80% of the day occupied with oral or composed communication.

The requirement for communication abilities is significant for all intents and purposes for each vocation. Professionals in Big Six bookkeeping firms invest 80% of their work energy speaking with others, independently and in gatherings. Similarly, engineers burn through the greater part of their professional lives composing, talking, and tuning in.

Communication capacity can bring about the better possibility of advancement

Specialized individuals with great communication aptitudes win more, and the individuals who are frail communicators endure. William Schaffer, a worldwide business advancement administrator for PC mammoth Sun Microsystems, made the point vehemently: "If one aptitude's required for success in this industry, it's communication."

Over 90% of the workforce officials at 500 US businesses expressed that expanded communication aptitudes are required for success in the 21st century.

Endorsers of the Harvard Business Review evaluated "the capacity to impart" as the most significant factor in making an official "promotable," more significant than aspiration, instruction, and limit with respect to diligent work. Research spreading over quite a few years has reliably positioned communication abilities as critical for administrators.

One twenty-year study that pursued the advancement of Stanford University MBAs uncovered that the best graduates (as estimated by both professional success and pay) built up their communication aptitudes by picking courses, for example, business composing, driving, convincing, selling thoughts, arranging, talking with, directing gatherings, settling clashes and working with social assorted variety.

Preparing workers in communication for improved profitability

The National Commission on Writing found that American businesses burn through 3.1 billion dollars (roughly R30 billion rand) yearly preparing individuals to compose. At any rate 80% of organizations in account, protection, land and administration survey composing abilities during their contracting forms.

A portion of the businesses overviewed said they paid for composing preparing programs for salaried representatives with composing wasteful aspects, featuring the requirement for compelling working environment communication.

In a meeting with the "New York Times" Bob Kerrey, executive of the National Commission on Writing, stated, "Composing is a 'marker' of high-ability, high-wage, professional work.

Individuals incapable of conveying what needs be plainly recorded as a hard copy farthest point their chances for professional, salaried work."

Regardless of whether you are contending to land the position you need or to win the clients your organization needs, your success or disappointment depends to a huge degree on your capacity to impart.

If you figure out how to compose well, talk well, listen well and perceive the suitable method to convey in different business settings, you'll increase a significant bit of leeway that will serve you all through your vocation. Additionally, because your communication assumes a key job in endeavors to improve productivity, quality, responsiveness and advancement, your communication influences your organization's success.

BRILLIANT TIPS TO IMPROVE COMMUNICATION IN THE WORKPLACE

In about each part of life (both professional and individual), powerful communication is essential to success and satisfaction.

Connections can't flourish without open communication, and the equivalent goes for businesses, both enormous and little.

The nature of a business' inside communication often says a ton regarding the organization itself. When poor communication goes unchecked, your association's days might be numbered.

Luckily, there are a lot of ways you can improve communication in the work environment, a large number of which can be accomplished through your inward communications software.

1. Check-in with representatives all the time.

Checking in with representatives is basic for viable communication in the working environment. Plan face to face or online gatherings like clockwork or months, to talk about activities, issues, and the association overall. Does staff have suggestions? Grumblings? General considerations? Workers need to impart their considerations and insights. By regarding and esteeming your staff, you will improve communication in the work environment.

2. Strategize an onboarding procedure for new workers.

For more up to date representatives, it very well may be difficult to get familiar with the ropes of an association and how it genuinely works. Since most organizations work from a specific arrangement of inner learning, there's generally a worked in preparing program available to you. Make interior information effectively accessible by means of documentation and preparing recordings on your intranet organization. Likewise, ensure staff has refreshed worker profiles and Q&A gatherings are stuffed with data. Along these lines, new individuals can without much of a stretch discover individuals and answers, and you'll keep compelling communication streaming.

3. Evaluate your current inward communication methodology.

It is difficult to improve something if you don't have the foggiest idea about what's keeping you down. Communication techniques, for example, email, phone, informing, and in-person communication would all be able to fill important needs with their one of a kind advantages. Be that as it may, some might be more valuable than others. Email, for example, is most likely not the ideal approach to have a discussion with somebody. Numerous associations are supplanting email with social intranet software and joint effort devices. Make a rundown of your current interior communication strategies to figure out what's successful and what isn't. Thusly, you can make sense of where to roll out certain improvements.

4. Execute social intranet software.

When endeavoring to improve work environment communication, social intranet software is a top arrangement. Involved with apparatuses that streamline day by day business forms, an intranet additionally includes a powerful worker communications stage with simple to-utilize joint effort and discussion instruments. It engages representatives to interface and offer thoughts in a sans judgment condition. The ubiquity of social intranet software is developing at an exponential rate and is just winding up progressively natural to help each part of a business.

5. Have an "open entryway" arrangement.

Having a genuine exchange with chiefs and CEOs is one of the greatest communication deterrents workers face. They may feel uncertain about offering significant considerations to the chief, and accordingly, obstruct the progression of successful communication. Having an "open entryway" strategy where your workers feel good drawing anything out into the open, whenever, can be tremendously gainful to your business' interior communication and make you increasingly receptive. It is additionally an incredible method for propelling representatives in your association.

6. Make inside records and information effectively accessible.

Communication isn't generally individual-to-individual or individual-to-individuals. It's additional data. Regardless of the activity, record the executives and information sharing are indispensable to ordinary errands and you need your workers to discover documents, photographs, answers, and so on effectively. Your organization intranet will bring together this data and put it on the fingertips for your whole association. If you're attempting to improve communication, start with how staff finds what they have to carry out their responsibilities.

7. Exploit internet-based life.

Internet-based life is a ground-breaking help for businesses to speak with clients ... be that as it may, it can likewise improve communication in the work environment. Urge workers to like, remark, and offer intriguing presents that relate to your association. You can likewise utilize social instruments inside your intranet to receive the rewards of web-based social networking inside the ordinary movement of your business.

Enable representatives to impart their inclinations to one another to make important, business-related discussions. This is an extraordinary method to consolidate relationship-working with your business' objectives and ways of thinking.

8. Sort out your areas of expertise.

If discovering office data is a cluttered wreckage, you can't hope to have compelling communication in the working environment. Utilize your intranet to arrange divisions, and the individuals and data inside that branch, into a decent spot for workers to discover and get to. Office heads can likewise quickly speak with individuals by sharing reports and sending refreshes through a notification framework. You need a framework that is immediate – the executives ought to effortlessly have the option to contact individuals, and individuals ought to effectively access reports, data and higher-ups inside an office.

9. Make an inward language.

In some cases, the ideal approach to improve work environment communication and your representative commitment methodology is to make an inward language. This could incorporate abbreviations/monikers that are utilized each day to portray parts of the business, to a large group of made-up slang words propelled by your organization's inside jokes or standards. It's a fun method to keep things fascinating consistently and can no uncertainty improve the progression of compelling communication in the working environment.

10. Identify a shared objective.

Inside each association, there's a shared objective that drives your business. By identifying, clarifying, and fortifying this goal, you'll strengthen your staff's profitability by disposing of disarray with attachment. All things considered, there's nothing more significant for a group than for everybody to be in agreement.

11. Reward employments all around done.

When desires are set, individuals can convey. Perceive your representatives' endeavors when they go well beyond in an assignment or exceed expectations in a venture. The effects are twofold. In the first place, it recognizes and remunerates great conduct. People like to get acknowledgment, particularly when they buckle down towards an objective. Besides, it sets a model for different representatives, or at the end of the day, it conveys desires through activity. There are two or three different ways you can do this... if your intranet has gamification devices, you can reward focuses when individuals complete errands or send "identifications" when they lead extends successfully. Obviously, there's additionally the great good old in-person visit.

12. Convey an inward bulletin.

When stir grabs, it's difficult for workers to watch what's going on in your association. An inward pamphlet is a fantastic technique for sharing organization news and communications, regardless of whether it's little or great in nature. Ordinarily, week after week interior pamphlets are best, yet you can explore different avenues regarding how often you drive them out. Abstain from over-burdening inboxes with messages and house the bulletin in your intranet.

13. Adjust your office.

If you're working in a physical office, probably the ideal way you can improve communication in the work environment is by reworking the plan. You'll need to stay away from the run of the mill workspace or segment arrangement, which can separate representatives and put a damper on successful communication. Modifying your office to an open floor plan will welcome representative communication and joint effort, also make the space increasingly pleasant to work in.

14. Round out worker profiles.

Successful communication in the work environment is almost inconceivable if the staff doesn't have the foggiest idea about who's who. Worker profiles will take care of that issue. Urge representatives to altogether round out their worker profiles in your intranet. This goes past giving a name and email. Staff ought to likewise transfer a photograph, include individual interests, and rundown groups they are a piece of. Regardless of whether your business is huge, little, or totally remote, attentively finished profiles will manage discussions and associations.

15. Concentrate on organization culture.

Organization culture ought to be available in your association. This is the means by which you interface workers with one another and adjust them to your association's objectives. You can do this by conceptualizing worker commitment thoughts or making an infectious aphorism. Likewise think about marking your social intranet, office style, and business documentation, among other security. If there are any center ways of thinking that your business encapsulates, don't spare a moment to emphasize them all the time.

16. Get outside of the office.

Going through hours and weeks on end in the office can have negative mental impacts on everybody – particularly during the colder months. Here and there, everything necessary is a difference in view to liven individuals back up. Getting outside the office doesn't mean burning through significant work time. Propose a lively coffee look for your group to work or present intermittent work-from-home Fridays.

17. Calendar a work retreat.

Discussing leaving the office, there are times when you should interrupt business-related movement and calendar a fun group trip with your representatives. Work withdraws, for example, picnics, climbing excursions, or scaled-down golf, are brilliant alternatives. These exercises ease individuals from stress and improve inward communication in the working environment by allowing individuals to unwind. Remember that retreats and worker commitment exercises don't need to spin around work. Easygoing exercises can restore your office and structure nearer bonds.

18. Permit your representatives the chance to energize.

Working extended periods of time can be debilitating, physically and rationally. Everybody has encountered it... when you're understandingly consumed, it very well may be difficult to discuss adequately with others. Offer your representatives the chance to take required breaks. Regardless of whether this implies longer snacks or periodic individual days, you'll show signs of improvement results when you release a stale situation and enable workers to reboot.

19. Strengthen associations among directors and workers.

In numerous associations, directors and representatives work intimately with one another. This isn't the situation for each business, notwithstanding, and it's normal for workers to have snappy associations with administrative staff. By empowering more grounded cooperation among representatives and chiefs, you'll actually direct more grounded communication in the working environment.

20. Have a confided in the HR division.

A few organizations have a difficult time making their HR divisions a spot staff needs to go to. It's fantastically amusing because a human asset office exists to help the people who work for you. Communication in the working environment will enormously improve if your area of expertise that handles inward concerns and arrangements is trusted by everybody. Ensure the HR workforce is agreeable, mindful, and effectively available. (Your intranet is the ideal spot to unify HR for your whole organization.)

21. Try not to rebuke blending.

For certain directors and CEOs, a water cooler visit appears sat around and cash. This couldn't possibly be more off-base. Representative blending is a basic part of relationship-building and you can't anticipate that individuals should become more acquainted with one another if they're just talking about work. If your workers want to blend and have an off-subject discussion or discussion, let them.

22. Debilitate single direction communication.

Numerous businesses adopt a top-down strategy to communication, which has been a great technique for a considerable length of time. Single direction communication controls your message, however it won't serve you or your representatives over the long haul. Rather, make an open line of communication for workers – you'll see various advantages by adopting this strategy. Keep in mind, communication is a two-way road.

23. Continuously share significant news.

If you need solid communication, you have to impart when it is important most, for example authoritative change. Regardless of whether the news is lovely or difficult, it's significant you articulate the data truly, when you can. Here and there, this message is best conveyed by a CEO, different occasions, another authority individual. These are choices you have to make previously. Continuously have an arrangement and be available to exchange from staff.

24. Organize a steady substance creation.

Making online journals and wikis will strengthen information sharing for inside and outer gatherings in your association. By urging your workers to make and distribute quality substance, you'll be enabling them to have a voice in the organization, which all by itself is a type of improved representative communication. In addition, representatives can "like" and remark on their colleagues' posts — another powerful apparatus for encouraging beneficial dialogs.

25. Show intranet content on screens.

If your office has screens in the structure, use them to share data from your intranet. This is a simple and unobtrusive approach to connect workers with news and drench them in your organization culture. You can communicate up and coming occasions, workers of the month, or declarations. Now and then showing data in a different spot or configuration gets more footing.

26. Consolidate versatile advancements.

Like never before, individuals are utilizing cell phones and tablets for everything. Since numerous representatives wind up outside of the office all the time, you need work available on cell phones. A versatile intranet will take care of every one of your issues. Regardless of where workers are, they'll have the option to access archives, individuals, and data.

27. Go to meetings as a group.

Pretty much every industry has its own arrangement of gatherings consistently. Going to meetings as a group is a magnificent method to open up communication and adapt together to how your association can push ahead in your industry. Similarly as with a retreat, gatherings are extraordinary for group constructing, and can be monetarily stable if arranged ahead of time.

28. Utilize a CRM stage.

Whenever clients are included, ensure your workers have the best business communication devices to speak with them. Utilizing a CRM stage is an extraordinary method to track tickets or request, which will quicken turnaround time for client service. Without solid apparatuses, endeavors could be copied, client requests could go overlooked, and your client maintenance will endure.

29. Track errands.

A composed record of errands, due dates, and need levels ensure everybody comprehends what they ought to do. This is especially useful when overseeing numerous workers. Utilize your track chief apparatus in your intranet to effectively allot and record ventures. Continuously live by way of thinking that if it's not recorded, it doesn't exist.

30. Timetable status gatherings.

The more you can monitor groups about their errands and current activities, the better. You can have day by day or week after week status gatherings face to face, through video chats, or on the web... what's more, they don't need to surpass 10 minutes. If everybody's situated in a similar time zone, attempt to plan a gathering for a similar time each morning. These gatherings will evacuate negligibility and improve communication in the work environment.

31. Direct stay interviews.

You may ponder... what is a stay meet? Stay meetings are one-on-one gatherings where directors, or others in an administration position, visit with representatives to make sense of what's working or not working in their occupations and the organization all in all. The objective is to forestall undesirable turnover, improve communication in the work environment, and find what necessitates fixing. In some cases a stay meeting can be the answer to your issues.

32. Identify and connect with modest representatives.

Regardless of how you cut it, a few people are modest. Self-observers are in no way, shape or form a plague, truth be told, they're similarly as significant and proficient at what they do as forceful workers. Contact independent individuals and have agreeable discussions where they can share their thoughts. You can't improve communication in the work environment if you are feeling the loss of a gathering of representatives. Remember: this can be a protracted procedure and modesty doesn't disperse medium-term.

33. Support video conferencing for remote workers.

When you're overseeing remote representatives, relationship-building can be difficult. One answer to this very normal issue is video conferencing.

It's as face to face as you can get. Timetable week after week video gatherings to examine business-related points or appreciate group building exercises. (Moment emissary, worker profiles, and movement streams are likewise some social intranet instruments that abbreviate the separation.) This is an incredible method to become more acquainted with the consultants you work with, particularly if you plan on enrolling their administration's long haul.

34.   Utilize   mysterious   proposal discussions.

It might sound old fashioned, yet proposal boxes are another approach to improve communication at work. Go the virtual course and set up a discussion on your intranet where representatives can share concerns, regardless of whether it's an insignificant point or significant concern. Individuals aren't constantly open to being vocal however are bound to do as such if they can adopt a mysterious strategy.

35. Worth collaboration.

Numerous representatives like to deal with activities exclusively because they don't feel great teaming up with other individuals. This is the hindrance you're attempting to kill. Stress the significance of collaboration consistently. Requesting that your representatives taking group-based (as opposed to solo) methodologies may cause introductory uneasiness, yet a couple of psyches are in every case superior to one.

36. Take stock of your own communication abilities.

Each CEO needs its workers to impart adequately, however shouldn't something be said about your very own aptitudes? There's consistently an opportunity to get better and particularly in positions of authority, you have to adjust sentiments and take analysis. The ideal approach to fill in as a model chief and improve communication is by continually taking self-stock and re-surveying your very own inside communication procedure.

37. Be friendly.

Unbending conditions don't profit anybody. Obviously you need an objective situated organization that exceeds expectations in your industry. Yet, to genuinely have successful communication, you should be affable... you should be human. Open entryway arrangements, stay meetings, and friends excursions are incredible strategies to improve communication, however if your vitality is cool, these endeavors may crash and burn. Have a go at breaking several jokes, grinning every so often, and ensuring discussions are two-way boulevards. The exact opposite thing you need is undesirable conditions where representatives fear coming to work.

38. Commend birthday events and commemorations.

We've talked about how agreeable conditions improve communication. The key is to treat workers as individuals. Reporting birthday events or work commemorations are little signals that fabricate a people-arranged network and make staff feel esteemed and acknowledged. Post a little declaration on your intranet or host an organization lunch-in. You'll discover individuals will open up when you look into their lives.

39. Send studies.

Despite the sort of association you run, each worker is different. Send a study asking your representatives how they like to get data (through the social intranet, email, face to face gatherings, and so forth.) to help actualize the best communication plan. This is a simple method to pose direct inquiries and all the data will be logged consequently. Moreover, your staff will welcome that you care about them, which looks good for worker spirit.

40. Welcome inquiries.

We have a truism here at Axero Solutions: "If you have an inquiry, inquire. If you believe it's senseless, inquire. If you think you know the appropriate response, solicit." Questions are one of the most central parts of powerful communication in the work environment. Similarly as you ought to pose inquiries, so should your representatives. Impart that outlook in your association. Ensure workers are agreeable to connect with inquiries to you, chiefs, or one another... particularly when slip-ups happen.

41. Commend your accomplishments!

Improved worker communication benefits your whole business. Pause for a minute to celebrate what you've accomplished after you've placed in the work. Gather information about expanded execution and profitability so you can impart to the organization and set new objectives.

Improving communication in the work environment is a steady work in advancement. It is a give-and-take relationship that requires persistence, care, and the capacity to tune in. There are numerous methodologies you can take, however when you take them, you'll see a lift in worker commitment and efficiency. Utilize the above tips to make a network inside your association that develops and succeeds, together.

CHARACTERISTICS OF EFFECTIVE BUSINESS COMMUNICATION

We have all been there. The business meeting where everybody contributes with their sentiments and nobody takes any notes. The following month there is a subsequent gathering that comprises similar talks with the exception that the members have spent the whole month winding up more genuinely contributed, and still there is nobody taking notes. After a year similar dialogs proceed, and we hear it expressed that, all proof in actuality, there is progress. We scratch our heads and attempt to have an uplifting standpoint that things are pushing ahead. Email, SMS informing, voice, internet-based life, and even the tricky up close and personal gathering. With the numerous types of moment communication open to the undertaking, one would figure our endeavors at business communication would be faultless. But then, in one way or another, despite everything we neglect to convey compelling business communication and the effect to the business is acknowledged in postponements, re-work, cash, and political repositioning.

The shortcoming appears to lie in the supposition that whatever media we pick, it will some way or another convey the message we need to pass on with little speculation from the sender. With such a significant number of choices open to us by means of innovation, we appear to have dismissed the essential ideas driving business communication.

Communication, when all is said and done, requires planning, thought, and some approach to affirm that the message was gotten in nature as well as in comprehension. Business communication can be considerably increasingly unpredictable. The accompanying five points are a speedy survey of the characteristics that are fundamental for powerful business communication. How about we tally them down:

5. Plan

Wikipedia states that an arrangement is a graph or a rundown of steps with subtleties. We plan our closets; We plan our excursions; We plan house redesigns; We make a basic food item rundown; and we plan supper. But then, for reasons unknown, when it is important to pass on a message of significance with respect to corporate assignments, expectations, or business destinations, we bounce in, lips first and don't take the time required to really consider the message it is that we need to pass on. Compelling business communication requires arrangements ahead of time.

To get the beneficiaries' consideration, start a communication with a brisk explanation in regards to the explanation and significance of the message. Is this about a key deliverable that lines up with the corporate vital arrangement? Does it kill an effective hazard? Try not to leave individuals scratching their heads, misconception, and maybe in any event, overlooking the message because the significance of the message was not clarified rapidly.

We live in a time of moment gratification. If the purpose behind, and the significance of a message, isn't passed on and seen rapidly, you will have lost your group of spectators. Plan what you need to state and express the key message right off the bat in the communication.

4. Expel feeling from the room

Forcefulness; intensity; dread; outrage; sicken. There is no place for feeling when it comes to settling on a successful business choice. When individuals talk straightforwardly from feeling, they often miss the target while energetically demanding they see the target more plainly than the remainder of the room. Business issues ought not to be interpreted as close to home destinations. If this is clear, it is imperative to isolate the individuals from the issue. That is a key message of intercession and arrangement. In all actuality, consistently in business is an activity in intervention and arrangement.

If you need to convey a significant message, and there is considerable feeling in the room, you are ideal for conveying the message at a different time and maybe even invest some energy reevaluating if you even have the ideal individuals in the room.

3. Be brief

This is especially significant in composed communication. Today, numerous business exchanges are exclusively led by means of email. A couple of key slugs are considerably more compelling than a few run-on sections. We should likewise not disregard the standards of accentuation we learned in evaluation school. The universe of SMS content informing doesn't pardon us from utilizing accentuation and isolating points into sections.

On account of face to face gatherings, phone calls, and video-conferencing, guarantee that the sessions end on schedule. If you plan your message well, there ought to be no motivation to expand the session past the foreordained time. Be brief in the conveyance of your message. Something else, the message you need to convey could be lost as members search through your words and reach their own determinations or even separate and begin to make their supper arrangements.

2. Development

The human cerebrum is a bustling organ. As we are tuning in, we likewise will in general process other information that is haphazardly meandering around back to front heads. Tragically, we are not as great at handling different information similar to the specialized gadgets we get to. Continuously expect that the beneficiary of your communication might shuffle numerous undertakings as your message is being conveyed. Because of this, it is critical to offer some sort of follow-up toward the finish of your communication. Consider finishing a session with an announcement, for example,

'We will plan a subsequent session in about fourteen days. This will offer everybody the chance to process the new corporate destinations and we will be available to any inquiries or remarks around then.' Sending meeting minutes with errands, proprietors, and due dates is likewise a best practice, as is catching up with a real composed communication following any foyer dialog of significance.

1. Tune in

We've heard it previously, and I'll state it once more. The top normal for powerful business communication is tuning in! None of us are radiant to the point that individuals need to hear us out pontificate! It is disturbing and incredibly incapable, also an extremely speedy approach to losing regard.

I invest quite a bit of my energy gathering data from business partners through round-table sessions. Luckily, I can console quick and I utilize this expertise to catch significant articulations and key messages that are spoken during those sessions. There are times when even my flawlessly sharpened keyboarding abilities can't keep up, and when that occurs, I stop and request that the individual recurrent their announcement. Most occasions they don't recollect what it is that they just stated, yet they are very glad to keep talking.

Stop and think for a minute. If you can't rehash the last three sentences you just talked, you might just pontificate. Fortunately it is very conceivable to figure out how to listen more and talk less, and the outcomes are quantifiable in the extremely present moment.

In this day and age of moment gratification, we risk dismissing the significance of compelling business communication. We bounce in with no foreknowledge, arranging, or thought of the message itself and the beneficiary. Successful communication requires exertion, and by setting aside the effort to get ready, alongside holding fast to these essential characteristics we can guarantee that we are creating positive associations with our representatives, our business partners, and our partners.

THE EFFECTS OF POOR COMMUNICATION IN BUSINESS

Communication is an unavoidable truth, particularly in the work environment, where collaboration, innovation and remote work are progressively normal. For a business to flourish, comply with time constraints and surpass objectives, strong communication frameworks and connections must be set up. When stress, neglected desires, social breakdown, low resolve, disappointed customers, family issues, wellbeing concerns and a littler primary concern become ceaseless work environment issues, poor communication could be at the foundation of the issue.

Worry in the Workplace

High-feelings of anxiety in the working environment are a tremendous sign that there are communication issues. Poor communication can make an inclination that everything on your plan for the day is critical, making you and others rush, feel tense, exhausted and have practically no comical inclination. Great communication causes a feeling of soundness and consistency, yet the absence of communication or unfortunate communication presents a feeling of dread that causes pressure, which is counterproductive to effectiveness.

Workers who are focused on throughout the day return home worried and worn, which effects their families. Rather than having a life partner or parent who is vivacious and appreciative to be home, the family is left with somebody who has such huge numbers of feelings to empty from the workday that a night is scarcely sufficient opportunity to get it hard and fast. Representatives may start to feel remorseful or even to experience struggle at home because of their strain and anxiety. This pressure remains with them as they start the following workday and it very well may be hard, if certainly feasible, to excel.

Neglected Needs and Expectations

The absence of communication causes neglected desires. Groups miss cutoff times, customers miss arrangements, and individuals on a task don't appear to comprehend what their jobs are. When workers experience difficulty making sense of what their needs ought to be, they often pick an inappropriate thing and wind up disillusioning their bosses. Without unmistakably conveyed desires and needs, it is difficult to realize where to begin and how to finish an undertaking effectively.

Contentions and Other Relational Breakdowns

If you have ever opened your work email inbox, just to locate an accusatory message from a partner, worker or chief, you have most likely encountered the feeling of disappointment, outrage, hurt, dread and defenselessness that can accompany undesirable working environment communication. Rather than posing inquiries about how a venture is tagging along or what your needs and objectives are, the email peruses in an accusatory and requesting tone.

Your already positive relationship may feel stressed, so when you pass your associate's or manager's workspace, you are probably going to need to cover up, as opposed to plunk down and have an amicable arrangement discovering discussion. You may even feel a feeling of vulnerability about looking for compromise because of a paranoid fear of how it may influence your employer's stability. It is additionally basic to feel a feeling of instability or absence of satisfaction in finishing your day by day errands, and these feelings hinder profitability in the work environment.

Low Morale and High Turnover

When individuals are managing exceptional feelings, they invest more energy than ordinary on enthusiastic administration. Profitability goes down, and confidence is supplanted by a positive feeling of enduring the day. Work environment endurance mode can be a genuine issue. When business connections are injured and there is no fix, trust departs for good, making it difficult to cooperate in complying with time constraints. When individuals miss cutoff times, they will in general feel ineffective about execution. This endless loop keeps groups and businesses from arriving at their actual potential.

Physical and Mental Health Issues

When things are turning out badly both at work and at home, it isn't bizarre to encounter outcomes to mental or physical wellbeing. Psychological well-being concerns and ceaseless medical issues are bound to be created during unpleasant occasions, particularly when a representative has no outlet for stress help, is out of vitality for self-care, or needs enthusiastic administration abilities. When these issues spring up, support appropriate professional consideration and use it as a chance to pivot the circumstance.

Disappointed Clients

Disappointed customers can be an indication of poor communication. When groups miss cutoff times or arrangements, bosses will in general be disappointed and pushed, however do as well customers. If your customer depended on telephone administration to start before its fabulous opening and your establishment group missed the cutoff time, your customer could be out of cash. If your legitimate group isn't completely arranged to display a case in court and is making things up along the way finally, the decision probably won't be in your customer's support. When nursing staff misses a cutoff time, it could imply that a patient doesn't get a drug or a shower on schedule.

When customers are disappointed, they often take their business somewhere else, which costs your organization cash.

Improving Communication

If poor communication can effect feelings of anxiety, cutoff times, spirit, wellbeing and the main concern contrarily, then great communication can have a positive and recuperating impact. Work out employment and undertaking depictions plainly and register to ask how things are going. Utilize messages and informing applications carefully. Treat others with the generosity you trust inconsequently. Make a composed rundown of needs for times when there is more work than time, and maybe put aside time every week to straightforwardly address work environment concerns and conceptualize arrangements.

Practice undivided attention abilities with colleagues and accept the best of customer expectations. Make a culture of commending achievements and progress. When fitting, look for help from a corporate clinician or communications expert who can show your group communication, self-care, undivided attention and passionate administration aptitudes. Keep in mind that none of us have immaculate communication abilities, however by embracing a growth attitude and moving a positive way, upgrades can happen rapidly.

Regardless of how enormous your organization is, communication is an urgent factor in its success. An organization where great communication is rehearsed will in general be exceptionally profitable. On the other side, awful communication can have some grievous ramifications for your organization. How? Indeed, here is a portion of the impacts of awful communication in business:

Diminished Employee Motivation

Inspiration and confidence are basic parts of efficiency. When your workers find that they can neither speak with you or one another, they will probably experience the ill effects of an absence of inspiration. They may understand that they don't completely comprehend the main job. The poor communication in the association implies it's difficult for them to go to partners or even their bosses and request help.

The consequence of this is your workers begin to experience the ill effects of low confidence in connection to their capacity to play out the job needing to be done. In the long run, the activity will either be done ineffectively or not be done by any means.

Communication works the two different ways. It's a sort of criticism circle that streams from the business to the workers and back. As the business, you speak with the representatives, let them take a shot at what you've imparted to them, and get criticism from them on how successfully your directions were completed. An open-entryway condition where workers aren't hesitant to request clarification or give proposals is one in which the representatives are allowed the chance to develop certainty.

Diminished Employee Productivity

Any business will need to be beneficial, as efficiency improves the probability the organization will achieve its objectives. Gainful representatives are better ready to finish assignments and meet targets. A breakdown in communication, nonetheless, eventually prompts a breakdown in efficiency.

Poor communication may result from workers who aren't ready to discuss appropriately with their bosses, or they're not able to discuss well with one another. It likewise might be that the objectives of the association and the errands identified with them are not all around imparted. In such examples, efficiency will be decreased because of an inability to impart.

Clear communication with your workers empowers them to be all the more likely to comprehend your needs and needs as an association. Ensure they comprehend your authoritative objectives well and the undertakings they have to do to accomplish these objectives. An open entryway arrangement additionally guarantees that they can generally request clarification and present issues to the senior administration early enough. This most optimized plan of attack ventures and builds efficiency by and large.

Expanded Mistakes in the Workplace

Another impact of poor communication is the absence of comprehension. If you don't let your workers completely comprehend what is anticipated from them, they are probably going to misjudge their obligations. This normally prompts more slip-ups in the work environment, which thusly prompts diminished efficiency.

A typical guilty party in this regard is your composed communication. Ensure it is clear and surely known by your workers. Tell them that they can generally request clarification if they feel uncertain about anything. The equivalent applies to your verbally expressed directions too.

Communication is about as essential to the success of your business as capital or the business' item. With great communication, your business can scale new statures of profitability you didn't envision conceivably. Without it, your business will before long wind up floundering in its very own cesspool creation.

The issues that poor communication can make are often not understood until after the issues happen when business and the reality endures, but then they could have been anticipated.

Here are **4** fundamental issues that accompany poor communication:

1. An absence of knowing prompts pessimism

When individuals don't have the data or information they believe they need, low efficiency results. The explanation is really essential—individuals will in general stay away from circumstances in which they will be viewed as not knowing, not understanding or not having mastery. Nobody needs to appear as though they don't have the foggiest idea of what to do. Furthermore, pretty much everybody has a dread—regardless of whether situated as a general rule or not—of being humiliated or derided.

Recall school; From an opportune time through graduate school, how often did you hear instructors and professors state, "There's nothing of the sort as a moronic inquiry?" They realized when somebody had an inquiry—a generally excellent inquiry that would help shed new light on the discussion—that they were essentially too reluctant to even consider asking.

2. Representative doubt, non-appearance and low confidence

Representatives need to be locked in so they feel associated with the association. When they will be, they are happy to work more enthusiastically, more brilliant, and be dynamic in the work environment in manners that drive business results. When they aren't locked in, when they don't feel associated, they endure.

This may appear to be an unstable feely, soft business issue, yet despondent and separated workers can profoundly affect business through truancy, absence of inspiration, and turnover.

3. Terrible relational connections

How often do you see eyes roll? What amount of murmuring do you discreetly hear? When individuals don't feel associated with one another, it opens up the entryway for distortion, and for addressing thought processes and purpose. The absence of inclination regarded or tuned in to—really tuned in to—drives individuals to feel nullified. When that occurs, they often discover approaches to "push back," in any event, when they can't do it straightforwardly or legitimately.

4. The "Grapevine Effect"

Marvin Gaye isn't the one in particular who's heard from other people. Regardless of the amount you may, when workers are locked in and motivated they drive...love his Motown hit, you don't need one of these developing in your association. However, by not sharing data, you are guaranteeing a grapevine will grow—causing issues and interruptions. Individuals need what they can't have, and they normally expect there is something to be had if they're not demonstrated differently. If you aren't speaking proactively about issues that are critical to your representatives, the odds are that another person is—paying little mind to the precision and honesty of their "data."

As the Prince of Soul serenades, "I wager you're thinking about how I knew, about your arrangements to make me blue. It overwhelmed me I should state, when I discovered yesterday. Don't you realize that I heard from other people... "

Something will be shared by somebody, it just won't be what you would state. Maybe it won't be right.

So if there are every one of these drawbacks, for what reason aren't we imparting better?

It's not as though the board comes to work every day saying, "I need to retain data." Likewise, representatives don't state, "I need to mess something up!" So, what's at play? Much of the time, it begins with our convictions about communication that disrupt the general flow. Keeping us away from enormity are convictions and dread.

We accept we are brought into the world great at conveying and subsequently don't rehearse and don't beat that.

We're apprehensive about coming up short, and that dread prevents us from difficult and adapting new things or aptitudes.

We have a mixed-up conviction that great communication is all "presence of mind."

We erroneously expect others to comprehend what we know.

To truly address the drawbacks of poor communication, to get to the numerous upsides of viable communication and quicken our business results, we need to look at our convictions and, now and again, change them.

Improving communication includes something beyond spreading the message appropriately with the goal that it's heard (however that by itself can be a test). It means guaranteeing that the message resounds with and is comprehended by the listener(s) such that it will move them to activity. It's diligent work, however it's justified, despite all the trouble.

Poor communication is tremendously affecting the working environment. This as indicated by the "Communication hindrances in the cutting edge working environment" study as of late discharged by The Economist Intelligence Unit and supported by Lucidchart.

As indicated by the examination, "misty guidelines from bosses, silly gatherings and different stressors can snowball into bigger issues with broad effects on the business."

Respondents state poor communication is prompting:

- postponement or inability to finish ventures (44%)
- low resolve (31%)
- missed execution objectives (25%)
- expanded pressure (52%)
- lost deals (18%)— some value countless dollars

Poor communication resembles an infection – it begins little and duplicates, in the end spreading and contaminating the whole association's money related wellbeing.

To address poor communication, organizations must comprehend the main drivers. The three most much of the time referred to reasons for poor communication, as indicated by the investigation:

1) Different communication styles (42%)

As indicated by the investigation, almost 33% of twenty to thirty year olds (31%) state they utilize texting at work each day, contrasted and just 12% of people born after WW2. The issue with utilizing innovation to impart is it makes more open doors for miscommunication or bombed communication. As we feature in The Bullseye Principle, email or messaging evacuates non-verbal communication and vocal elements from the communication condition, further decreasing the chances your crowd will get your message, as planned. That is because composed messages don't pass on conventional expectation signs, for example, outward appearances and vocal tone. That expects your beneficiary peruses the email. One investigation discovered 60 percent of individuals who get an email read just 50 percent of the message.

The arrangement: impart enthusiastic messages face to face.

2) Unclear obligations (34%)

Not realizing what to do or who is answerable for what causes pressure. The most widely recognized spot this occurs? Gatherings. As indicated by an examination, center supervisors spend up to 35 percent of their time in gatherings and senior level officials spend up to 50 percent. The vast majority of these gatherings are inefficient. When inquired as to whether laborers leave gatherings with an unmistakable comprehension of the following activity thing, 46 percent of members replied: "a portion of the time," "seldom," or "never." Not actually an empowering reaction.

The arrangement: decrease the number of individuals in your gatherings (eight or less is ideal) and make an arrangement of responsibility and characterize specific, quantifiable, time sensitive subsequent stages for participants. Representative assignments and get affirmation that participants can and will convey.

3) Time weights (31%)

Time weights make pressure because most aren't prepared to give it. When feelings are high, it ends up difficult to think unmistakably. We shift into "battle" mode and our barriers go up. When this occurs, our minds get over-burden and we respond sincerely before the reasonable piece of our cerebrum has gotten an opportunity to consider the words we simply let out.

The arrangement: practice care. Care decreases pressure, improves memory and directs dread or nervousness. To control a minute where you feel overpowered, pursue a straightforward procedure we call Stop-Breathe-Look-Listen. When you begin to feel surged or on edge, recognize your sentiments and acknowledge they are substantial. Stop whatever assignment you are doing and center altogether around your breath. Breathe in through your nose for about five seconds and after that breathe out through your mouth for five. Look. Notice all that you see and get notification from the buzz of the climate control system to the garbage in the wastebasket. If you feel your consideration begin to drift or interruptions begin to pull you away from your present minute, set your attention back on your breath and let it ground you.

Communication among laborers and supervisors affects the degree of profitability and employment fulfillment seen inside an association. Poor communication can prompt the absence of group union, misty informing, sat around idly assets, harmed connections, low representative spirit, higher turnover rates, lost income and even damage or passing.

REPRESENTATIVE ENGAGEMENT BEGINS WITH COMMUNICATIONS

Representative commitment is an intriguing issue nowadays, and it is all well and good. Only 33% of representatives view themselves as "locked in." Why would it be a good idea for you to mind? Higher working environment commitment prompts an about 40 percent decrease in non-appearance and 21 percent higher efficiency, also what it accomplishes for client support. Ever conversed with an irritated client assistance rep? Dreadful. It was in October that we found out about the disappointed 9-1-1 administrator who was impolite to guests, yet put their lives in threat.

While most client confronting workers don't have a client's life in their grasp, they do significantly affect how that purchaser sees the organization. Helping workers feel esteemed is one stage in boosting representative commitment. Another progression is engaging them with the correct devices, data and assets to carry out their responsibilities well.

It's not astonishing that 50 percent of representatives state that managers sharing data and information has a significantly positive effect on efficiency and inspiration. Know what else is important? When representatives can share data and information among one another. The majority of this takes a certain something – communication. Think communication is consigned to individual connections? Investigate why worker communications matters.

6 Effects of Poor Employee Communications

1. Diminished Cross-Collaboration

33% of workers express the capacity to team up makes them progressively faithful. How would we work together? Through loads of communication and sharing of thoughts and information. It's normally not the absence of capacity to team up that is the issue. The greater part of us figured out how to cooperate with other people back in kindergarten. The issue is that numerous associations don't give current coordinated effort instruments that make teaming up simple.

It is ending up progressively uncommon to work in an office where everybody works in a similar area, during those hours. As we become progressively portable, a greater amount of us works remotely, making a face to face cooperation testing. Each association, especially those with any remote or voyaging representatives, must give a simple to-utilize, simple to-get communication and joint effort instrument to unite everybody, regardless of whether just practically.

2. Lower Morale

We needn't bother with measurements to realize that when our manager isn't imparting great or giving us great apparatuses to speak with one another, it tends to disappoint. There is additionally misconstruing, and less responsibility and strengthening. Things get missed, ventures get postponed and somebody gets accused. That is no real way to work and it's certainly not going to propel you to come to work every day and give it your everything. Thus, withdrawal.

Representative resolve accomplishes something beyond effect colleagues, it can have an overflow impact on clients. Actually, organizations who report the most elevated worker fulfillment rates often are among buyers' preferred organizations. Is it because upbeat workers are bound to put the client first? Perhaps it's as basic as simply feeling great magic at work makes you want to spread the affection.

Communication is the foundation of each relationship. Practically every investigation of connections destinations an absence of communication as the main source for separation as well as disagreement. You will most likely be unable to enable each worker to figure out how to utilize their words successfully, however you sure as damnation can give them a stage for which they can draw in with collaborators.

3. Diminished Efficiency/Productivity

We've often referred to the detail that 20% of the representative time is spent searching for data or individuals who can help. We utilize this detail because it is so basic in understanding where all the time is going. Isn't that an inquiry business pioneers pose to themselves routinely?

I'd state the vast lion's share of organizations is reliably and purposely searching for approaches to expand profitability while bringing down expenses. It's an essential ROI idea. If you need to take advantage of the ability you have, give them the devices they have to accomplish more. The 20 percent of their day squandered looking for individuals and data is the low-hanging organic products you can rapidly and effectively get back basically by giving them communication instruments that put the majority of that data readily available. Email isn't the appropriate response. It is the issue. What amount of time do you spend burrowing through messages and email chains, attempting to find a connection, perusing messages to discover who said what, or sending messages that take hours, if not days, to get a reaction?

4. Stifled Innovation

Something enchanting happens when individuals can convey and work together adequately... development is started. The ideation procedure for the most part takes more than one individual. Without a doubt, you may have an item virtuoso ready, yet most advancement includes numerous individuals assembling their heads to envision, to counter and alter one another, and to execute. These individuals may not be physically situated in a similar structure or even a similar nation. Do they have simple approaches to meet up?

Advancement takes innovativeness and creative mind, yet it additionally takes cooperation. Giving representatives a stage to convey, share information and thoughts, and to keep tabs on their development can just enlarge the imaginative culture organizations need to remain aggressive. It shouldn't be a torment to discover who in item advancement you have to converse with about your extraordinary thought. Put representative ranges of abilities, current ventures, involvement and accessibility in one spot where any colleague can without much of a stretch discover it to rapidly interface and see what that accomplishes for development.

5. Expanded Employee Grumbling

Griping workers is the same old thing. Endless TV shows and motion pictures satire such conduct. One thing that is generally new is the means by which expansive those grumblings can be. Before, one displeased representative may inform five collaborators regarding how hopeless they are. Today, nonetheless, online life puts an enormous amplifier to each worker's tirades, presenting organizations to a notoriety emergency.

Regardless of whether it be internet based life or an audit on Glassdoor, potential enlisted people are hoping to perceive what your workers need to state about you before they apply or acknowledge a position, 76 percent of them, truth be told. As indicated by Glassdoor, 33% of occupation searchers won't have any significant bearing to an organization except if it has at least three stars on its audit.

So what is the greatest grumbling workers have when it goes to their managers? The main issue seems, by all accounts, to be an absence of communication. This can be communication from officials to bring down positioning representatives, or between workers. Communication matters and your workers need to feel like they have open entryways and a viable communication stage they can access to interface with one another whenever.

6. Higher Turnover

It's unpleasant to be in HR nowadays. Worker turnover is at its most noteworthy in all cases. Regardless of the business, turnover is constantly an issue. Losing representatives, particularly after such a brief timeframe, costs organizations billions in lost efficiency; and expenses related to selecting, enlisting and preparing. Here are a couple of calming details:

- 41% of laborers beyond 50 years old have been with a similar boss for at any rate 20 years.

- 21% of twenty to thirty year olds state they've changed occupations inside the previous year, multiple occasions the quantity of non-recent college grads.
- One of every three specialists will change employments in the following a half year.
- 47% of workers are probably going to search for a new position in the following year.

However, the news isn't all terrible. Recent college grads who feel they are at an incredible working environment are multiple times bound to design a long haul future there. So how would you make your work environment an "extraordinary" work environment? As indicated by the expert on the issue, Forbes, "66% of an organization's overview score depends on the aftereffects of the Trust Index Employee Survey... the review poses inquiries identified with workers' frames of mind about the administration's validity, by and large occupation fulfillment, and fellowship. The other third depends on reactions to the Culture Audit, which incorporates point by point inquiries concerning pay and advantage programs and a progression of open-finished inquiries regarding enlisting rehearses, strategies for inner communication, preparing... ."

Brotherhood and inner communications are among the principal subjects that rank managers high in representative reviews. What actions is your association taking to encourage fellowship and communication? They go connected at the hip, you see. Email may help with communication, albeit cumbersomely, yet it does nothing to fabricate compatibility. Representative communication software can help with both because it is deliberately worked to do only that — give individuals a stage on which to impart, share thoughts, fabricate connections and encourage development.

JOB OF INTERNAL COMMUNICATIONS IN BUSINESS STRATEGY

An organization's business system is a basic archive that characterizes an organization's vision, targets, qualities and business model, and contains fundamental subtleties on how the business will stay focused and separate itself inside its industry. A reasonable business methodology is basically significant because it offers key data that will help direct and propel worker action. Also, conveying this methodology viably to representatives guarantees that every individual is effectively attempting to propel key objectives.

Representatives at each degree of the association must comprehend and exhibit the organization's key qualities for a business technique to work successfully. It's insufficient for upper administration to comprehend this technique; pioneers must have key lines of communication set up to appropriately disperse this data to other people, down to the bleeding edge workers.

Communications professionals must interpretation of the test of outlining every key purpose of the organization's business system and sharing these all through the association. The complexities of this assignment are the focal point of a course in USC's online Master of Communication Management program. Here, we'll investigate a portion of the center points shrouded in the course, including:

- How business methodology impacts an organization's everyday activities.
- Fundamental lines of communication that drive inward sharing.

- The risks of an ineffectively conveyed business methodology.
- The advantages of successfully scattering business technique.
- Successful techniques for accomplishing key arrangement inside the organization.
- A communications chief starts to delineate organization's interior technique.

The Business Strategy in real life

An organization's business procedure may begin as a smooth framework on paper, yet when these qualities are completely typified, they shape the whole substance of the association. Powerful inner technique communications will guarantee that representatives give a firm encounter starting with one area then onto the next, and it impacts everything from the tone and typography that is chosen by the promoting group to the kind of welcome that in-store workers offer when a client strolls in the entryway.

For instance, a key element of the business technique for the coffee behemoth Starbucks is the "third spot understanding." This alludes to how Starbucks has put itself aside as an enticing choice to work or home, where clients can settle in and make the most of their time.

Appropriately imparting the possibility of the "third spot involvement" to representatives is basic so they'll comprehend and welcome the estimation of the client who settles in with a PC. Workers won't surge guests away or treat them as if they ought to be out the entryway immediately when they comprehend this part of the business technique.

The Hazards of Poor Communication

Interior arrangement with a corporate procedure is significant to guarantee that workers' choices are eventually guided by the correct reason and formed by the organization's present vision. When representatives dismiss the organization's more profound products and long haul objectives, they can undoubtedly fall into an unremarkable daily schedule without a more noteworthy vision to drive them forward to new advancements and inventive techniques.

In numerous organizations, falling into any sort of routine is hindering to the hidden system of that business. For instance, at Apple, advancement is at the core of the business system. Notwithstanding, representatives likewise need to comprehend the business' concentration past the sheer push to push ahead. As Tim Bajarin clarified it in Time, "Ideologically, [Apple's] a working framework and UI organization first, equipment organization second." This is a basic qualification for communicators to make for representatives to center their endeavors properly.

Rebekah Iliff, Chief Strategy Officer of AirPR summarizes inside communications with a fascinating relationship. She noticed that vital focusing on is ordinarily utilized for outside communications, yet likewise features that "... when you consider it, 'inside communications' is simply promoting to workers. What's more, much the same as in customary showcasing, the more you cook your message to a specialty group of spectators, the more compelling it will be."

The Importance of Communicating Business Strategy Effectively

Productive communications' models are critical to any business today. A compelling procedure characterizes probably the most basic purposes of business tasks and ought to be taken care of carefully to guarantee that it's promptly open inside the organization. Communications professionals are entrusted with plotting the correct way for key communications.

The way wherein this is done will fluctuate by business, however there are a few significant methodologies that can be used. A communication professional may execute quarterly gatherings, bulletins or lounge blurbs to feature key purposes of the organization's technique and ensure these focuses are constantly upfront. The best alternative for any individual organization is a painstakingly custom fitted mix of communications that suits its very own corporate character.

Accomplishing Strategic Alignment

Communications Insights bears witness to that key arrangement must start with business objectives. The communications division is then liable for creating streamlined techniques for acquiring data on those procedures and objectives and separating it down to singular offices and pioneers. These pioneers ought to likewise be furnished with the correct devices and abilities to convey methodology viably to every representative.

Be that as it may, it doesn't stop there. Communications professionals are likewise accused of staying with everybody current on this purpose and center, in any event, when this can change every day.

The accompanying advances can upgrade interior communications and guarantee that the organization's procedure is being shared viably with representatives:

- Keep up cloud-based archives that framework the procedure.
- Slice back on email communications to drive more consideration regarding those that are conveyed.
- Make persuasive visuals that condense key focuses.
- Overview workers routinely to decide their mindfulness level with respect to the present business procedure.
- Actualize preparing programs that stress noteworthy approaches to execute the business procedure.
- Host interior occasions that typify and empower key corporate qualities.
- Specify clear methodologies for two-way communication with respect to business methodology, to such an extent that

representatives at each level have their voices heard and questions replied.

Getting your workers energetic about your business system will viably make each individual in the organization a significant brand representative who can help further the organization's objectives. As Koka Sexton, Sr. Social Marketing Manager in the past of Hootsuite and LinkedIn puts it, "When you can enact your whole organization to be brand diplomats, the full impacts of social selling can be felt internationally."

Communications professionals assume a basic job in initiating representatives as such. A successful way to deal with the organization's business system will bring about a profound draw in the representative base, where all activities are at last determined by the organization's basic beliefs and focused toward assisting fundamental inner objectives.

Sharpening Communications Strategy

A business methodology is just as successful as the representative execution that places it vigorously. A solid communications professional can help guarantee that basic methodology focuses are shared adequately all through the association, so representatives know about the business' general objectives as well as how they can add to best help these objectives. From teaching new contracts on the organization's guiding principle to sharing new methodologies successfully over the whole association, communications professionals are entrusted with keeping everybody well-educated regarding the system that is set up.

In reality as we know it where communication is always advancing, it's essential to remain current on the most recent strategies for conveying successfully to workers at all levels inside an association. Courses in the online Master of Communication Management program at USC Annenberg address the significance of interior business system communications, just as other key themes, including advertising, communications hypothesis and vital corporate communications.

MYTHS ABOUT EFFECTIVE BUSINESS COMMUNICATION

The capacity to obviously portray what you do, how it is different from every other person, and why your prospects should purchase from you is a basic piece of the success of any business. That is the reason an ever increasing number of businesses are turning towards calling the executives frameworks. When we offer a professional voice IVR, clients guarantee that their welcome messages mirror the character of their organization.

From the littlest email to the most costly notice, each bit of communication is a chance to frame an impression in your client's psyche. Be that as it may, would we say we are truly clear when we compose our business communications?

Reconsider. Take these 12 basic myths of business communications and test your (CQ) Communication remainder.

Myth #1 – The more data I can pack in, the better:

Have you at any point attempted to discover a needle in a bundle? It takes a great deal of persistence. Sadly, tolerance isn't something perusers of your business communications will have. If your message is covered in hills of content nobody will set aside the effort to look for it. Successful business communications center around a solitary message and dispose of everything else. Try being exact and to the point, it generally works.

Myth #2 – If I utilize huge words, individuals will believe I'm more astute:

Massive dialogue instigates an antipodal result. Utilizing huge words resembles a person with a costly sports vehicle, it very well may be seen that you are attempting to make up for something. Rather, go for short, clear, straightforward words that you would use in ordinary discussion. Your tone will be friendlier and your perusers will be progressively open to your message.

Myth #3 – By utilizing popular expressions, language and abbreviations, I'll demonstrate my industry information:

You should write in Shakespeare's language because that is about what number of individuals will really comprehend what you're attempting to state. Abbreviations are particularly destructive, so if they're important set aside the effort to explain them.

Myth #4 – Speaking about my significance will hinder others:

Have you at any point been stuck at a gathering with an individual who just won't shut up about how extraordinary they are? In addition to the fact that it is irritating it really is a major mood killer. Rather than gloating about yourself, accumulate tributes and enable your clients to brag for your sake. You'll discover prospects charmed and anxious to find out additional.

Myth #5 – I'll write in first individual so it won't bore:

The greater part of your perusers will have one inquiry in their mind when perusing your archive – "How might this benefit ME?" That implies, utilizing the Y-O-U word not the I (or W-E) word. Truly, there are times that a convincing account story can have an effect. Yet, as a rule, business communications ought to be about the customer, not about you.

Myth #6 - Follow the pioneer:

While it's constantly shrewd to gain from others, don't be substance to stay in the pack. Become a pioneer yourself by following your own head and heart.

Myth #7 - what's to come is out of our control:

Business proprietors, rather, should live by the well-known expression from the unbelievable Peter Drucker, the dad of the current administration, who stated: "If you need to anticipate the future, make it."

Myth #8 - Good fences make great neighbors:

In business, that bodes well just if you see your general surroundings as an adversary. Rather, consider it to be as your clam. Tear down the wall by shaping vital collusions with neighbors, organizations and different business people.

Myth #9 - When in uncertainty, consistently return to nuts and bolts:

If that implies accomplishing business as usual, it might keep your organization from getting itself out of its present wreckage. Now and again, changing course is the main way out to break the trench.

Myth #10 - You can oversee pretty much everything:

No, You can't. Practice your introduction, lift pitch or even that intense discussion you have to have with your chief. If you comprehend what you need to state already, you'll be increasingly successful conveying a reasonable message.

Myth #11 - Value in items and administrations compares to low costs:

A war pursued on the reason of undermining your rival is just a race to the base. Worth methods are meeting client desires and pointing higher so as to justify a reasonable cost.

Myth #12 - Watch the challenge intently:

If you're caught up with watching your back, you're not looking forward. That can bring about wasted vitality and assets. Concentrate on what you excel at and power the challenge to watch your back as you speed ahead.

There are a million different organizations out there, yet there's one thing they all share for all intents and purpose: They depend on communication to drive the business forward.

From basic beliefs to culture rehearses, compromise to selecting, sharing the correct message in the correct way is vital to running a successful organization. Regardless of this, we as a whole mishandle communication at some point.

Indeed, I've seen it firsthand at numerous organizations, including Zenefits, where I currently fill in as an HR Generalist on the inner HR group. As a colleague of the quickest developing SaaS startup in the U.S., I can say with power that it's similarly as insane as you would envision. However, I've likewise taken in a ton of exercises en route. The most significant one? The significance of communication in lessening strife and encouraging growth in your association. If that seems like a lofty objective, this is because it is. In any case, it isn't difficult if you get HR energetic about your endeavors, and begin to free your working environment of the riskiest myths in regards to individual communication. If you do this reliably after some time, you'll upgrade work connections and make room for unhampered growth for both your kin and your organization.

All in all, as a business head or HR professional, what myths do you have to pay special mind to? Peruse on for my main five myths.

Alisa's Top 5 Myths About Communication in the Workplace

Myth 1: "Business isn't close to home."

If your association is staffed by people, then your business is characteristically close to home. Savvy pioneers get this and skill to explore the unpleasant waters of human connection viably. HR can likewise assume a job in mingling this idea inside an association so administrators realize how to manage issues when they emerge. Here is a portion of my most significant takeaways:

- People need to interface. The more directors can interface with their reports, the quicker and all the more viably they can investigate clashes both enormous and little.

- Individuals are more than numbers or "headcount". It's anything but difficult to become involved with measurements and information focuses, yet understanding that every "worker number" is an individual with a life partner, a kin, a pet, etc, will enable you to settle on choices that add to association wide wellbeing.

- Safe specialists are increasingly compelling. As indicated by one of the mainstays of Leaders Eat Last, a stunning book by Simon Sinek, laborers who don't have inner feelings of trepidation in the group, gathering, or association level can concentrate on outside obstacles to survive. If you're proactive about giving powerful strategies to dealing with your staff, you'll spare your business from superfluous disarray when circumstances present themselves (and they will introduce themselves).

Myth 2: "What you state is the thing that individuals hear."

You never know precisely how your message will arrive with another person. That is the reason it's your duty to look at each conceivable confusion that may emerge in a circumstance before conveying a message. Distill your criticism or other HR data in the most straightforward of terms and discover numerous methods for saying it with the goal that the other individual gets it. It's likewise worth calling attention to that maxim that it, once, is typically never enough. Regardless of whether you're giving input to senior administration or supporting staff—or the other path around—be sure to repeat your message with the goal that you've been heard.

Myth 3: "Cash is the most significant thing."

Fat compensations don't take care of every one of your issues. Ask any HR professional, and they've likely had a director come to them sooner or later saying, "My worker appears to be so despondent however he gets quite a lot of money flow. I don't comprehend what the issue is." While it may not appear glaringly evident to certain supervisors, not all representatives care only about bringing home a major check. While compensation is as yet a top-worry for occupation searchers, especially twenty to thirty year olds, different variables add to misery at work, similar to group elements, organization culture, or struggle. If you're an administrator and you sense an issue, fight the temptation to avoid your representative, since this is typically the time you can have the greatest effect with an immediate report. Associate with your worker quickly and discover what's happening, or work towards revealing the issue in more than a few gatherings.

Myth 4: "The 'fact of the matter' is out there—and I know it!"

Remember that well-known axiom, "There are different sides to each story"? All things considered, it additionally applies to business settings, where I'd contend there is the same number of "facts" as there are characters in an association. Normally, clashes will emerge, yet when they do, it's significant for pioneers in the association to be aware of the way that there's constantly a component to the story you can't see, get to, or reveal. That is the place HR can assume a major job in giving direction to settling issues by first learning a timetable of the occasions that occurred. While you can't get to a solitary, conclusive "truth", you can go far towards conceptualizing goals that work for all gatherings engaged with a circumstance.

Myth 5: "Listening is simple."

So. Not. Genuine. Try not to trust me? Attempt to review when you went to a gathering without a PC before you, or a telephone in your grasp. Regardless of whether you think you were tuning in, the desire to define a splendid rejoinder or expansion to the discussion is consistently at the front line of your brain. The outcome? Baffling gatherings where divided thoughts are on rehash until time runs out and disappointments bubble over. Venturing into a gathering or 1:1 with the objective of listening more than you talk is probably going to bring about a more prominent comprehension of the gathering, and expanded hierarchical union.

Your Organization Requires Good Communication

As an HR professional, I accept that hierarchical success and positive business results require communication of basic data and input all the time. Maintain a strategic distance from detached tuning in by being amazingly present at the time: rework what individuals state to you and restrict it down to shared terms when depicting occasions, circumstances, and objectives. Comprehend that you may not ever know reality in a given circumstance. Relinquish the possibility that cash, regardless of anything else, keeps individuals at associations—I used to enroll and I've seen numerous circumstances where cash doesn't have any effect. Ultimately, recollect that there's nothing of the sort as 'over-communication'. By deserting these myths in the working environment (and outside of it!), it'll be a lot simpler to accomplish both HR and business objectives.

THE CHALLENGES OF BUSINESS COMMUNICATION

The capacity of a business to impart is critical to its success. From viably imparting strategies to staff to connecting with customers and clients, communication is a colossal factor in business tasks. There are moves intrinsic to business communication, in any case, not least that each technique for communication requires a somewhat different methodology.

Tuning in to Learn, Not Just To Respond

Potentially the most significant part of communication is tuning in. In any case, it might be exceptionally difficult for individuals to build up this aptitude. Because of the intrinsic weights of keeping up success in the business, there may not be an ideal opportunity to sit and tune in to the requirements of the representatives and the clients. Without really setting aside the effort to tune in and figuring out how to comprehend others' perspectives, administrative staff may never completely comprehend or know about the necessities, needs, disappointments and hardships of organization staff and clients.

Holing up Behind Technology

It is simple for businesses to depend too intensely upon innovation for communication purposes. Email, messaging, voice message and texting can be very powerful for the brisk exchange of accurate, direct data. In any case, the dependence upon this innovation to convey feelings can prompt and show a difference in the working environment. Businesses may find that communication through innovation spares time, vitality, and cash, yet up close and personal communication, particularly when the feeling is included, is a vastly improved channel of communication. Tone, pose, outward appearance and eye to eye connection can't be communicated successfully utilizing innovation.

Gatherings: Essential or a Waste of Time?

Numerous businesses are moving ceaselessly from gatherings as instruments of communication so as to spare time and to advance effectiveness. Representatives often consider gatherings to be time-squanderers. Regardless of the fact that it is so testing to utilize gatherings successfully, gatherings are a significant piece of working together. Gatherings can construct cooperation, making representatives feel a piece of something – in a perfect world, the organization. Gatherings are roads for laborers to give info and offer their suppositions. The basic test of utilizing gatherings in your business communication is making gatherings that are brief, educational, participatory and positive.

Side effects of Communication Issues

If a business is having difficulties with communication, notice signs create the impression that should trigger activity by the administrative staff. A few pointers are trouble, unreached objectives, an elevated level of mix-ups, throwing fault, low inspiration, low profitability, unsatisfied clients, contentions, high worker turnover and loss of customers. These can be manifestations of poor or hazardous communication.

Taking care of the Problems

It is conceivable to find a way to improve communication to defeat the difficulties that possess large amounts of business communication. As referenced, listening is high on this rundown. Use devices like reviews and remark boxes to support solid and classified input. Abstain from blaming one individual; rather take a shot at an issue with a whole gathering of individuals by utilizing proper preparing or directing. Those in positions of authority ought to have incredible communication aptitudes, be compassionate and common issue solvers.

If issues endure, a business may redistribute the issue to a nonpartisan moderator to determine the circumstance in an unprejudiced way.

Challenge #1: Rising Above the Noise of Everday Communication

Representatives are shelled by a wide range of methods of communication all through the workday, from telephone calls and messages to inward texting frameworks. Because of this, workers just have 3 minutes of steady concentration before an interference.

An intelligent survey during the online class found that most participants got office notifications through email, telephone trees, or by means of cooperation systems. Katharine contends that while these channels can function admirably to catch the representative's consideration, they need excess dependability. Mass notification frameworks that offer multi-channel communication with only a couple of snaps can guarantee dire communications ascend over the clamor of ordinary communication to arrive at workers.

Watch cut 1 of 5 to guarantee your basic business communications arrive at all representatives.

Challenge #2: Proactively Communicating With Employees

Most of the workers hope to get dire communications from their association with respect to crises. While it's significant for workers to get notifications about potential life-compromising occasions, opportune reports with respect to office terminations because of serious climate or framework blackouts should likewise be conveyed to guarantee business coherence. More focused on communication can advise specific groups about shift changes or remind divisions about refreshed HR approaches and enlistment cutoff times.

Katharine strolls through different work environment communication best practices and answers for communication issues in the work environment to appropriately notify your staff about a business disturbance. These incorporate appropriate information the board techniques, how to characterize arrangements for recurrence and level of communication, and guaranteeing you pick a basic communication stage that enables you to use pre-made informing layouts.

Challenge #3: Connecting with Traveling Employees During Critical Events

Area based alarming enables you to send specific and significant cautions to workers situated in influenced regions locally and universally. Katharine alerts associations from gathering freestyle reactions from workers during a crisis because those reactions become difficult to total and store.

Rather, she urges associations to search out communication stages that take into consideration further developed information gathering, for example, a surveying highlight, where reactions can be classified and collected, message conveyance can be followed, and activity things and directions can be incorporated. With this information, associations can send a subsequent alarm with much increasingly specific guidelines to the individuals who require extra communication.

Challenge #4: Receiving Actionable Feedback from Employees

Katharine says it's essential that associations give a vehicle to representatives to feel good revealing data. Representatives are on the bleeding edge and are the first to watch wellbeing, security, and office warnings. Enabling representatives to submit secret and careful tips with successful answers for communication issues in the working environment will caution your association to an episode in the near future, taking into account increasingly compelling alleviation and occurrence goals.

Challenge #5: Delivering Faster Resolution to Business Disruptions

By proactively speaking with representatives, guaranteeing that voyaging and solitary laborers are represented, and engaging your laborers to submit secret and attentive tips, your association is situated to give quick goals to business interruptions.

One significant recommendation Katharine gives is having job-based access controls for conveying notifications. Division level access can spread the duty of basic communication to different partners over the association to guarantee various communication plans are accessible if there should arise an occurrence of a business interruption.

CONCLUSION

Congratulations on taking this guide as you straighten your way to successful effective business communication. Communication assumes a significant job in each business and is one of the most significant abilities that decides the success or disappointment of a business. In this way, compelling communication is vital if you need to take your business to the following level. Also, to grow such abilities, aptitude advancement preparing is given.

Regardless of whether it is oral or composed, the absence of communication can enormously affect the efficiency of the organization. For this, your associations ought to consistently designate professionals that have superb communication aptitudes. Poor communication may likewise influence the business relationship, in this way prompting the disappointment of the business. In any case, to take care of the communication issue, you first need to realize how poor communication may affect your business. So here we have recorded underneath a couple of focuses that will enable you to comprehend the negative impacts of poor communication.

1. Lower effectiveness

The effectiveness of your association or a specific division can be impeded because of poor communication. The progression of work will be influenced by clueless introductions, dubious email messages or different archives with mistakes that will require revision. Along these lines, viable communication aptitudes are significant for the success of your business thus you ought to give employability abilities preparing to your group. Such abilities are vital for the successful finishing of a task, without which the fruition will be wasteful to finish.

2. Worker resolve

Business communication abilities inspire the representatives to work for better efficiency. To advance representative efficiency, an exceptionally shared and open condition is fundamental. The absence of communication abilities will demotivate the workers and they will need excitement to perform better. Likewise, it will unsettle the audience members as they will be compelled to endure exhausting introductions and tune in to guidelines that will rather confound them. This is the reason aptitude improvement preparing is important for better execution of the workers and for a more clear message.

3. Diminished development

An organization can contribute hugely to the advancement of the general public with its development. In any case, poor communication abilities can disable the limit and development of the organization to contribute decidedly to the general public. This is because just powerful communication can help in enhancing new thoughts. For this, employability aptitudes preparing is basic.

In this manner, you should have at this point acknowledged how significant great communication aptitudes are for the success of a business. Hence, the vast majority of the associations are offering to prepare for their representatives for better profitability and advantage of the business.

Compelling communication is critical to maintaining a business successfully. Great communication can charm you among your customers, increment your image picture among your seniors, and cause you to be respected among those who work under you. It can likewise help you in taking your business to the following level and procure you high profits. Then again, poor communication can confine the effectiveness of your organization. It might bring about missing fundamental business cutoff times, trickery in work forms, and above all can endure representative assurance. As indicated by an investigation led by Global English uncovers, "97% of representatives reviewed accept that poor communication because of deficient business language aptitudes can make misconception".

Often, there is a great deal of disengage in the communication procedure, which can demonstrate expensive to a business. It might be verbal misinterpretations, absence of cooperation, lost messages and vague writings or inadequately worded messages. Powerful communication - both inside and outside, increment association's viability, empowers smooth tasks and aides in decreasing business possibilities. Communication is for the most part of two kinds - Digital and Interpersonal. Here are some helpful hints to improve these two, which can profit your association and keep the things cruising easily.

Advanced Communication: Most of the business communication is generally done utilizing computerized medium, like email. Creating emails or texts is basic when we are dealing with a friend. The proposed intrigue bunch in business are corporate accomplices, so it's for each situation better to be formal. Undoubtedly, even a minor mistake made in your correspondence could conflictingly influence your legitimacy. It can achieve the loss of reputation and business as well. Coming up next are the basic centers you should seek after while drafting a business suggestion, email or distinctive business letters:

- Constantly treat messages like the honest sends, not simply the advanced letters. While drafting an email, utilize incredible words, build up a characteristic voice, move in the direction of your point and present a reasonable cutoff time.

- Art the email cautiously. Return, check and alter for greater clearness. Clean every single sentence to keep the communication straight, positive and compelling.

- Try not to put any off-base or hazy data. Check your realities before sending the mail. Any off-base data makes you look like you haven't completed your work.

- Do whatever it takes not to use any Emoticons, Colloquialisms and Slang, it may realize the loss of understanding and the individual scrutinizing your mail may not grasp what you are talking about. Keep it fundamental and to the point.

- Pick the best headline for your message. The title is the primary prologue to the substance of the message to the beneficiaries. Likewise, it helps in keeping your message out of the spam box.

- Furthermore, the most significant is to document all your business communication. Make envelopes to spare all the old messages. It will help you in finding any communication effectively later on.

Relational Communication: It is an up close and personal communication and includes trading data and the importance of means of verbal and non-verbal messages. Some of the time, an email or a book simply isn't adequate. Advanced communication doesn't include any immediate communication. No one sees you, but your composition; however, when you meet somebody up close and personal, numerous things, for example, your tone, non-verbal communication and eye-to-eye connection come into play. Your message ought to be clear, compact and direct to the point. Include underneath referenced tips in your relational communication to make it important:

- Be sure while meeting your customers or bosses and don't feel timid face to face to-individual gatherings. Keep in touch to establish a decent connection.

- Listen cautiously and give your total consideration regarding the discussion. Comprehend what the contrary individual is stating and after that give your very own contemplations.

- Concentrate on your discourse. Think before you talk and don't get mistaken for your own words. Doing this, will weaken the reason for the up close and personal gathering.

- Keep the communication professional, and abstain from making it excessively close to home. It's great to get to know individuals you are working with, yet don't make it excessively amicable.

- Never counter the assessment of your customer, regardless of whether you oppose their idea. It might offend them. Hear them out mindfully, then keep your perspective and clarify why you can't help contradicting them. In any case, guarantee to keep up a gracious tone.

- Pose inquiries to clear the entirety of your inquiries and concerns. It will in like manner help in having the dialog and will make new contemplations that would be valuable in business.

These were a couple of suggestions you can execute in your correspondence technique and make it successful. Following these won't just improve your business execution, but also it helps in making decisions that would be beneficial to your life. It will likewise help upkeep your confidence and basic leadership and also make you stand apart of the group. Successful communication is constantly about fathoming the other individual, not tied in with compelling your conclusions on others and winning a contention. This is why you need to ponder on what you learnt from this book and I promise you to build the best version of yourself.

Thanks for choosing to read this book.